MARTIAL

Maidens 2

COLORING BOOK

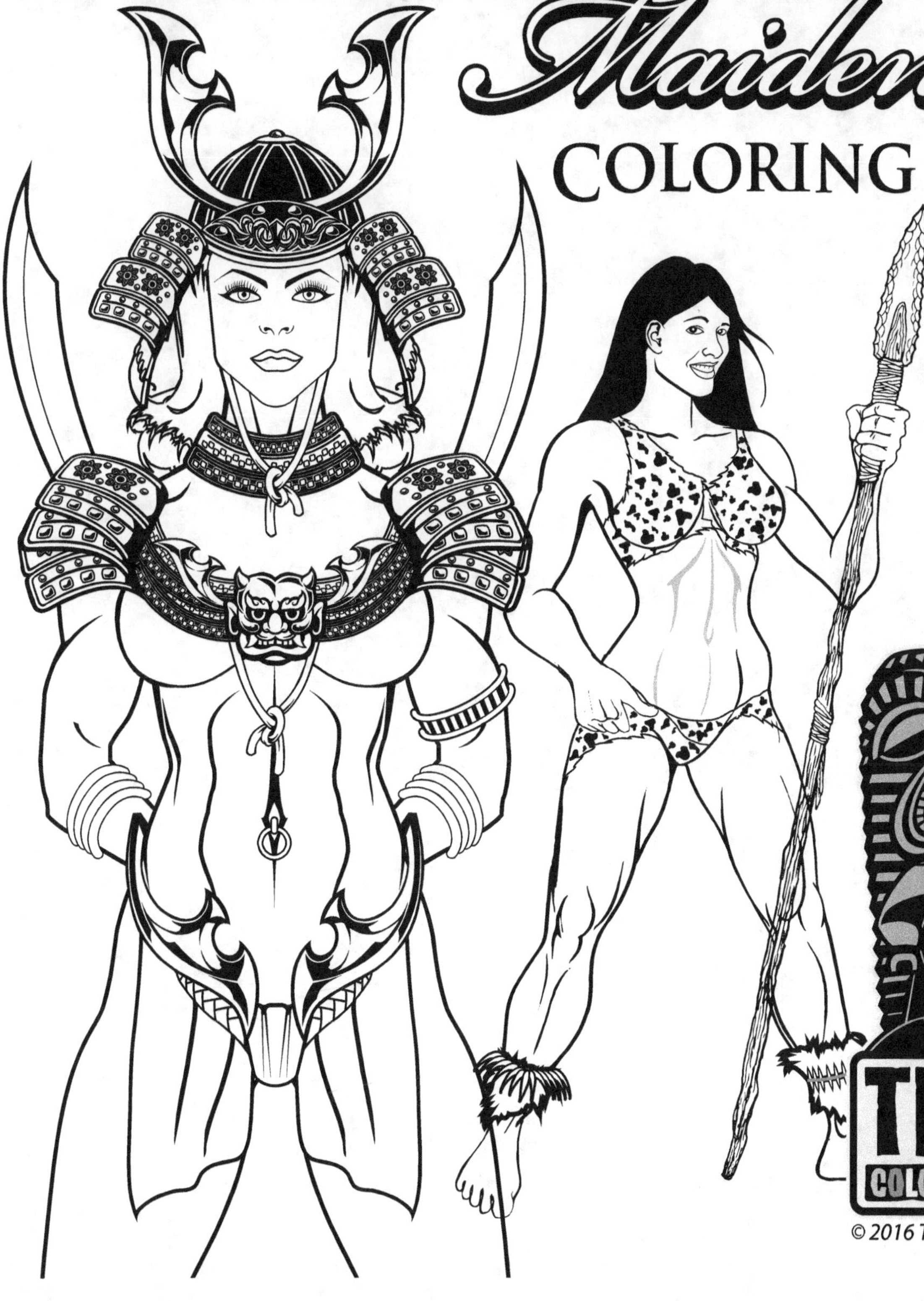

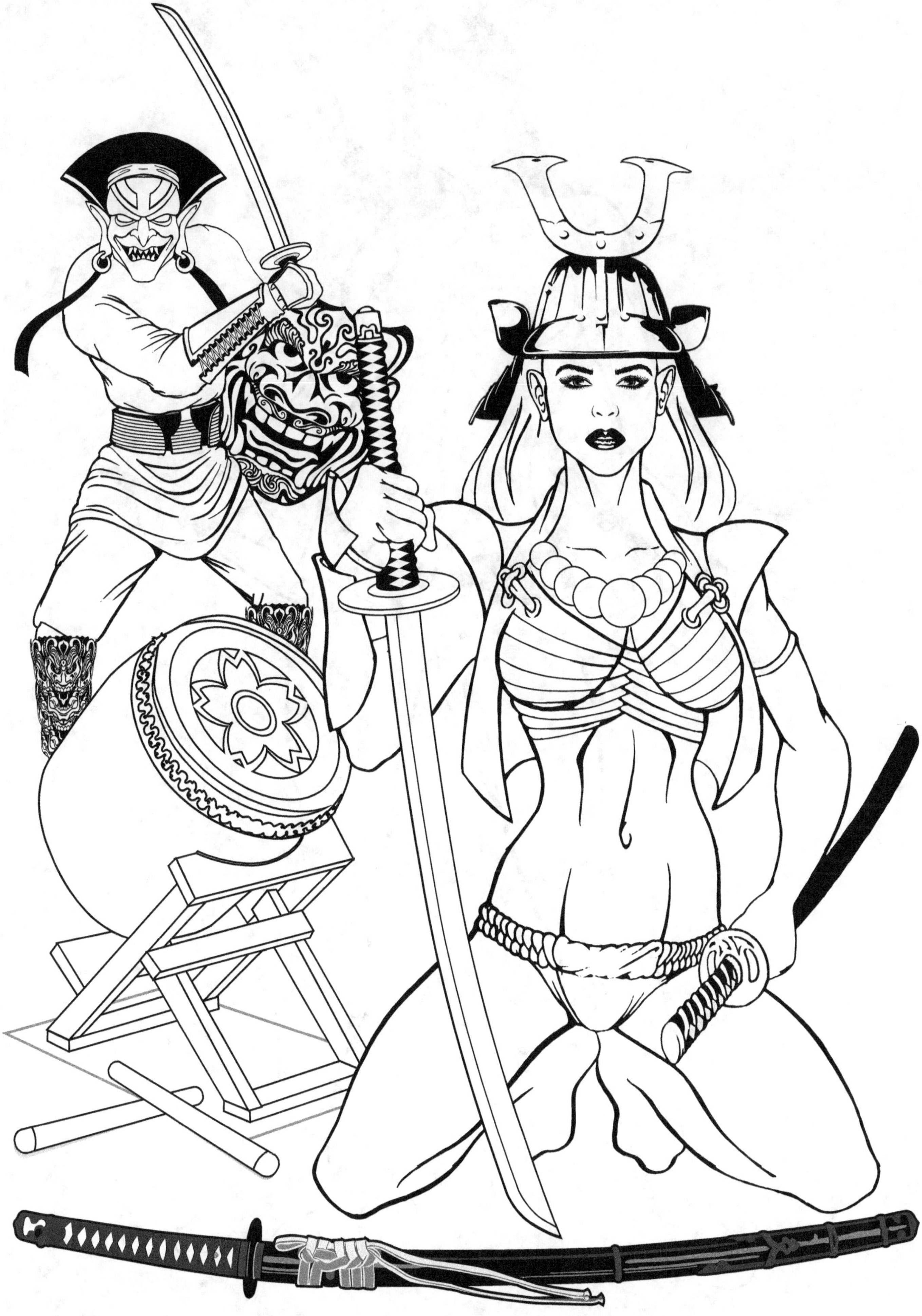

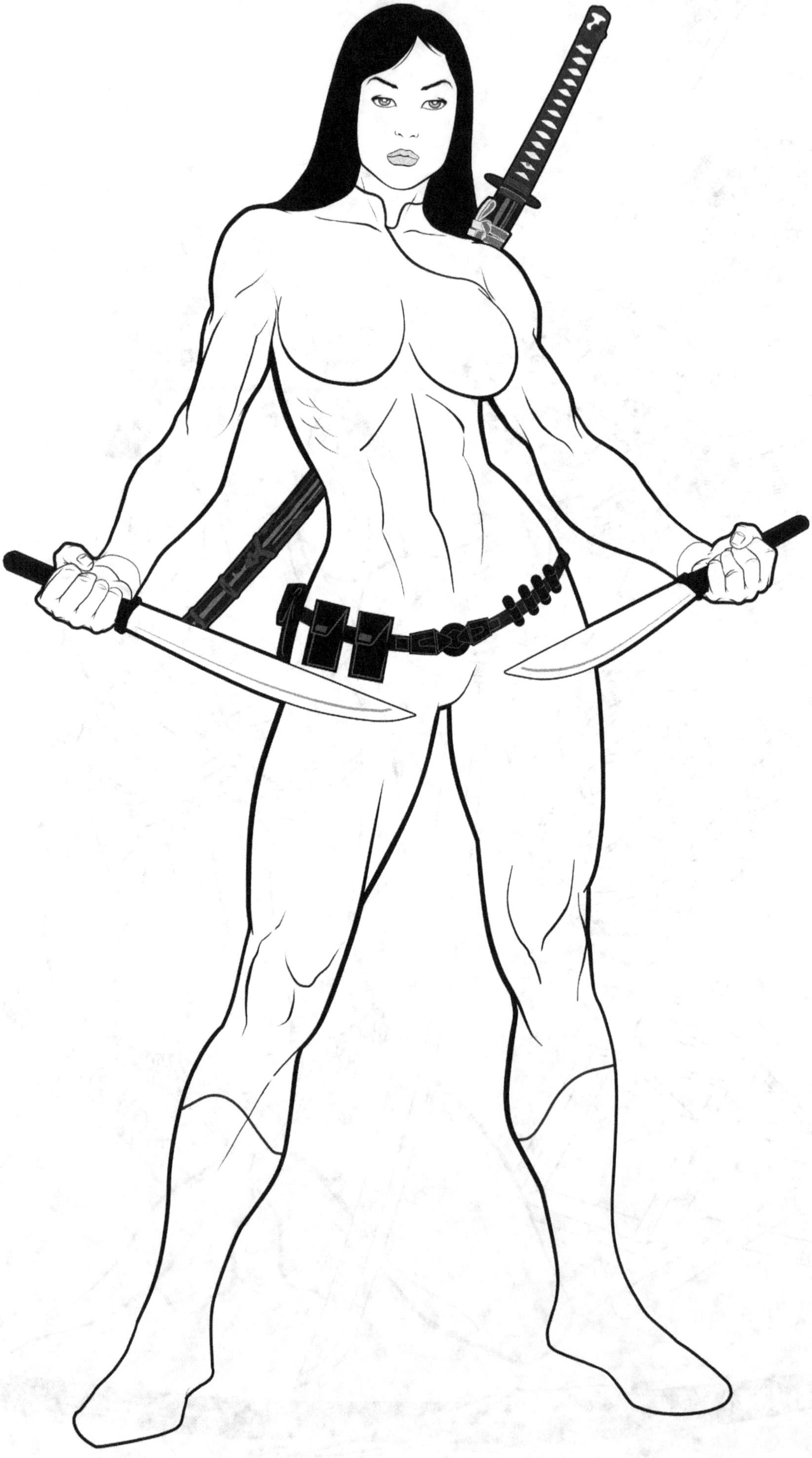

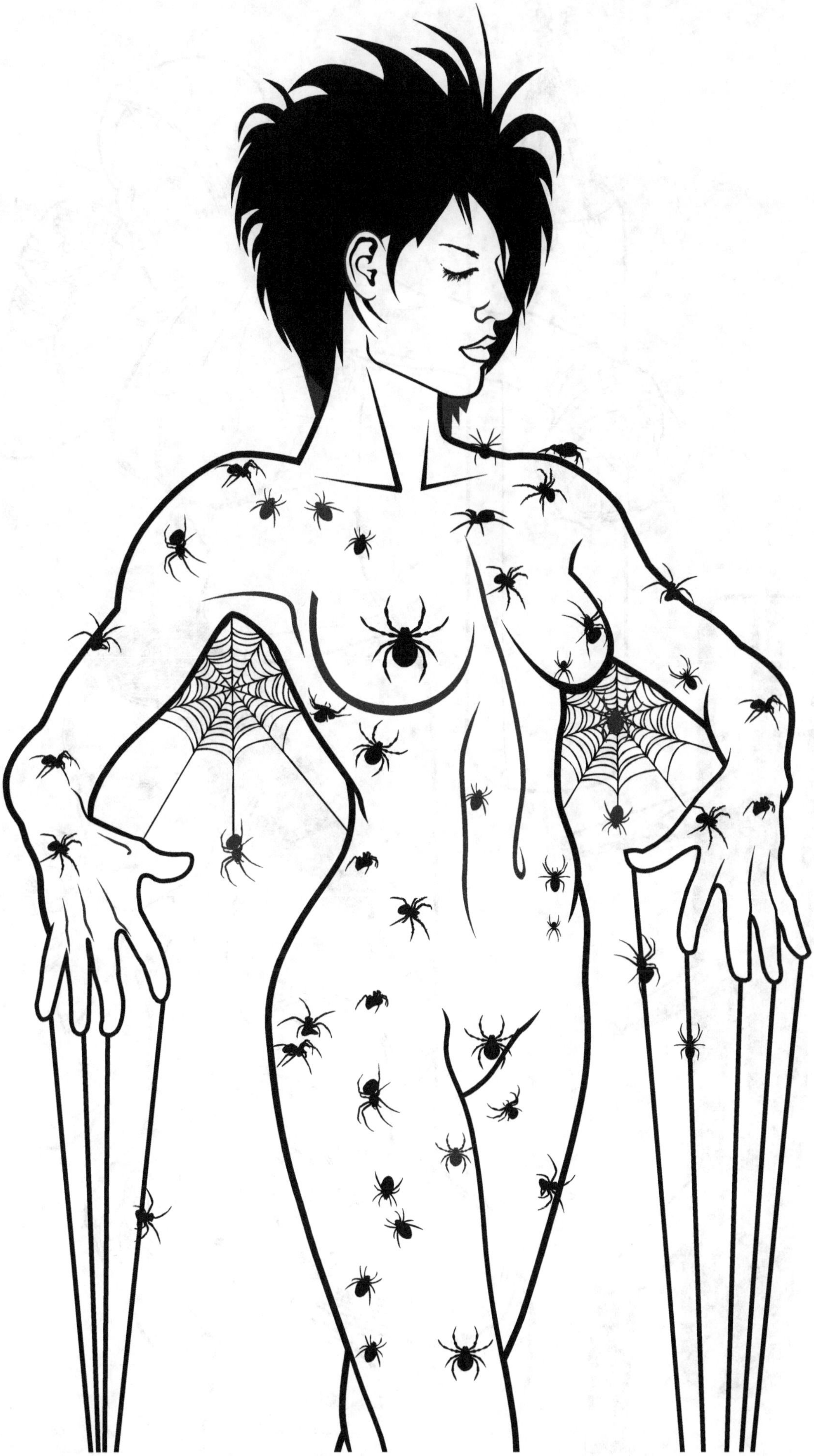

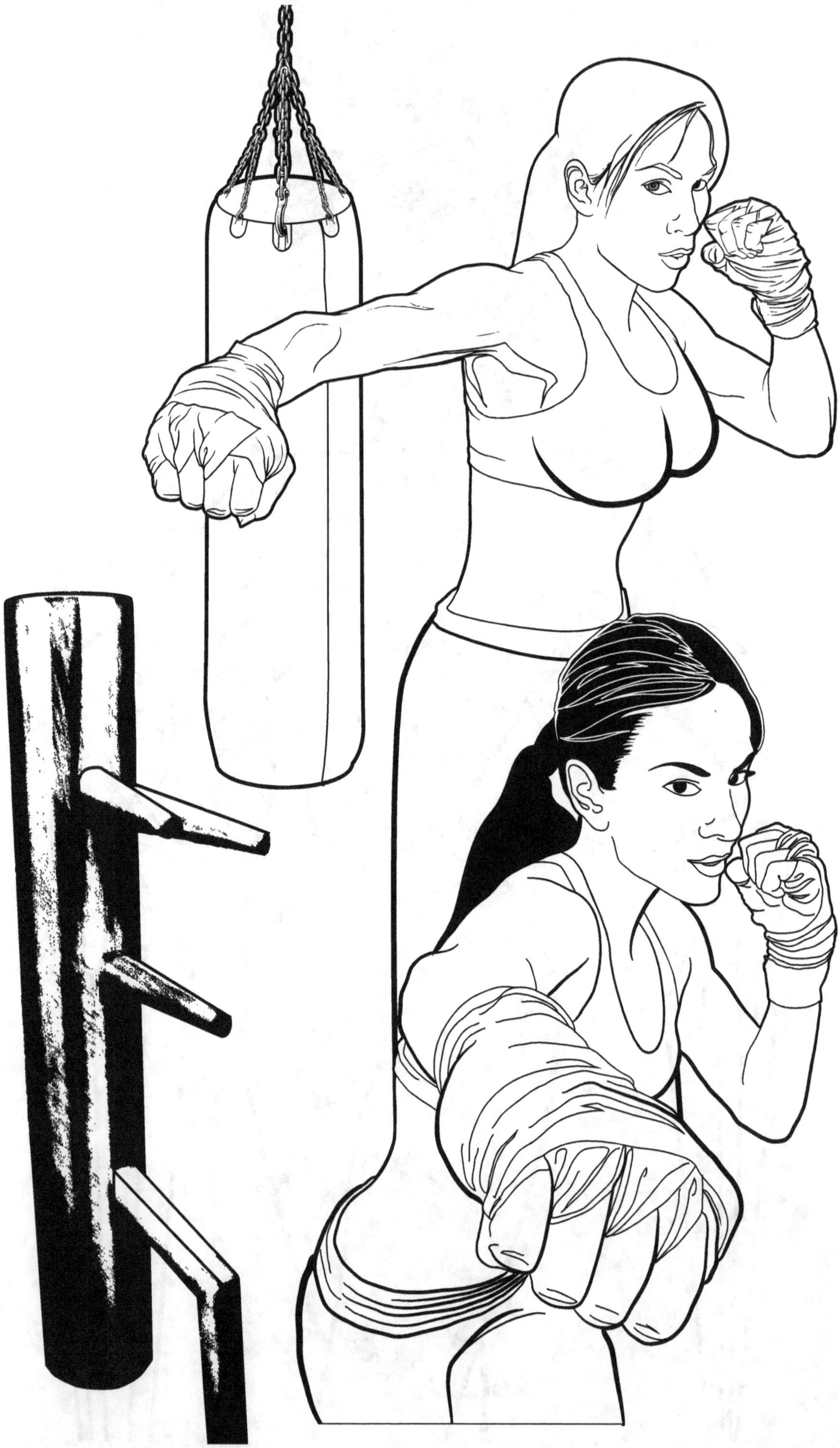

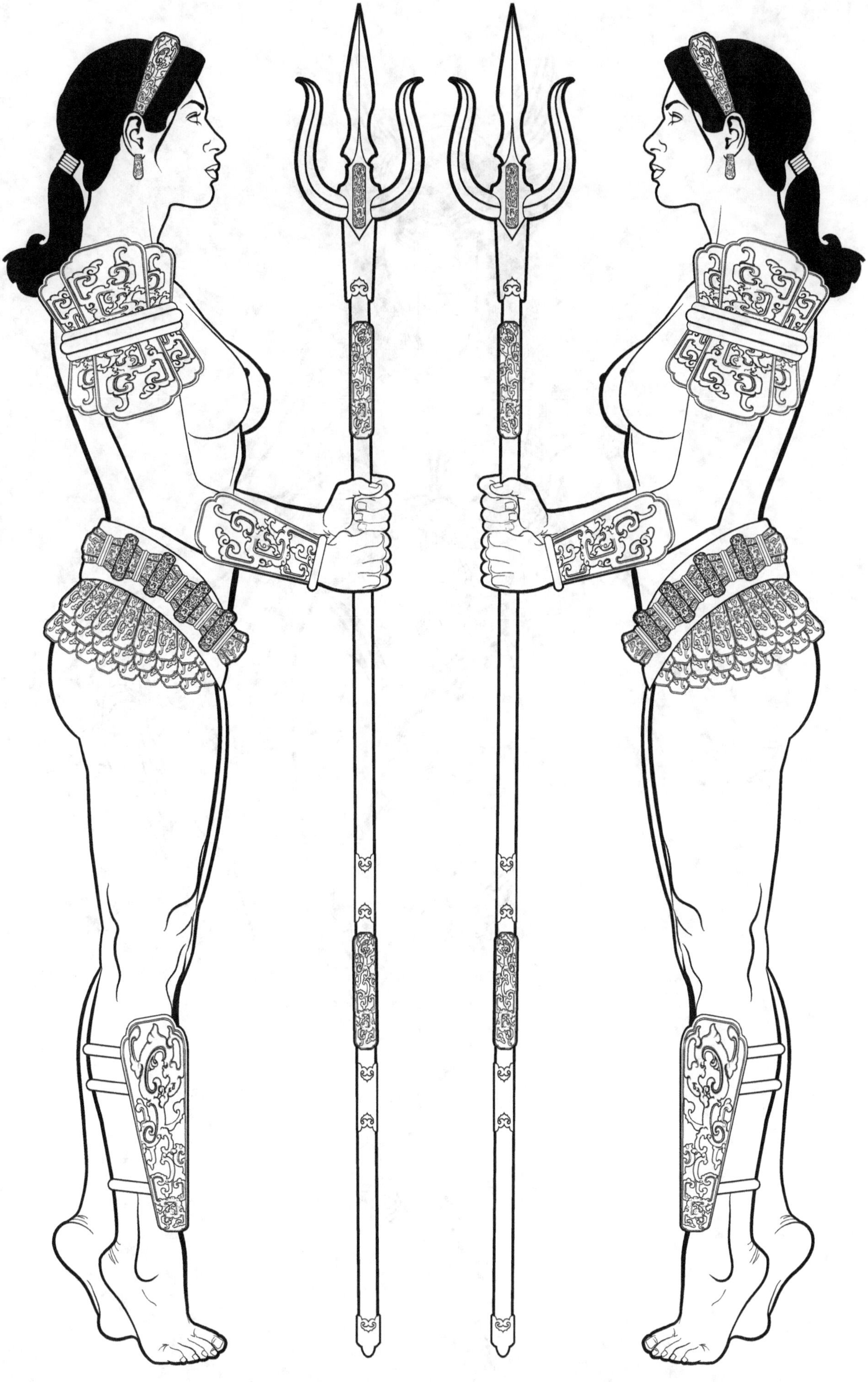

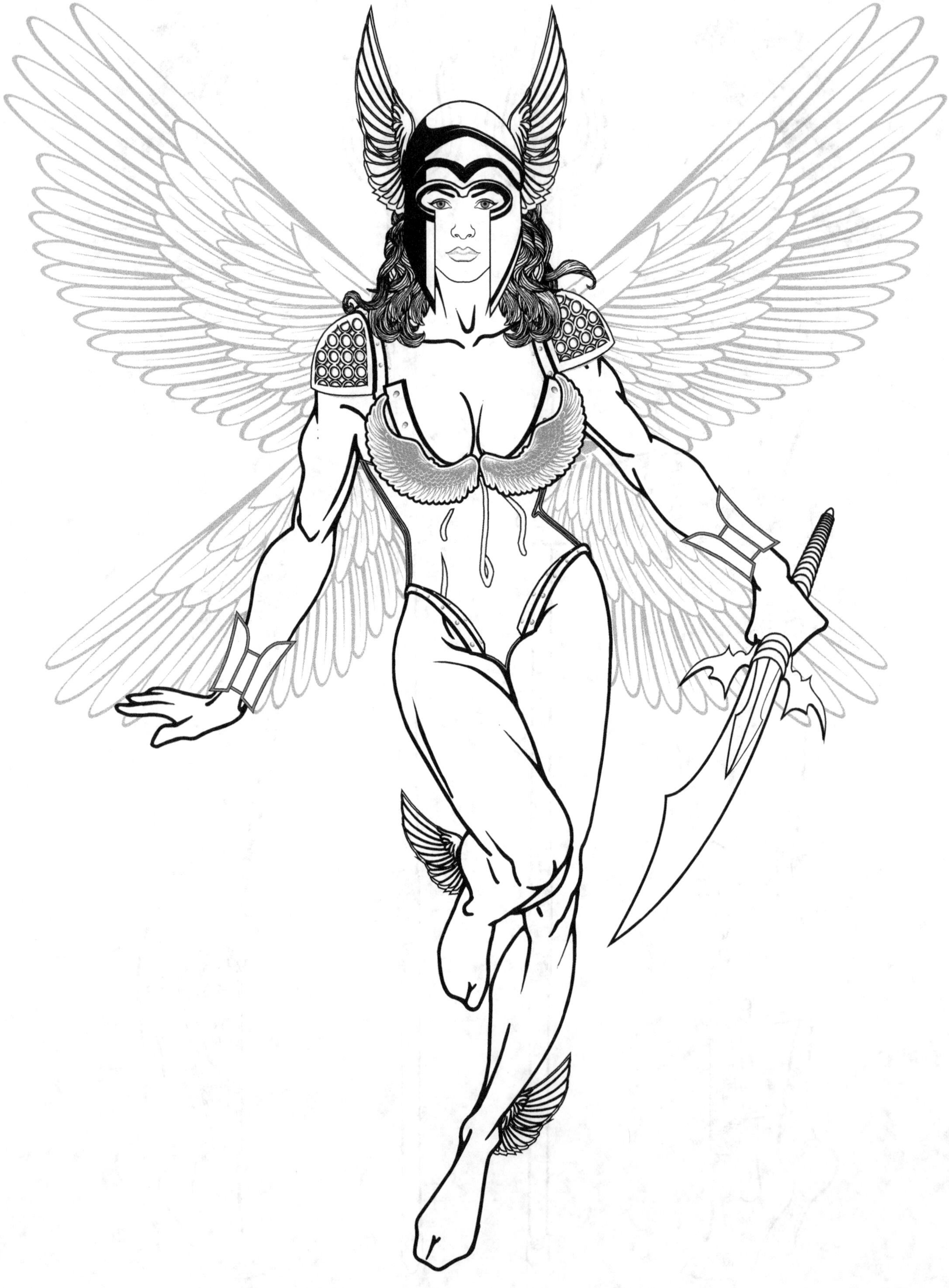

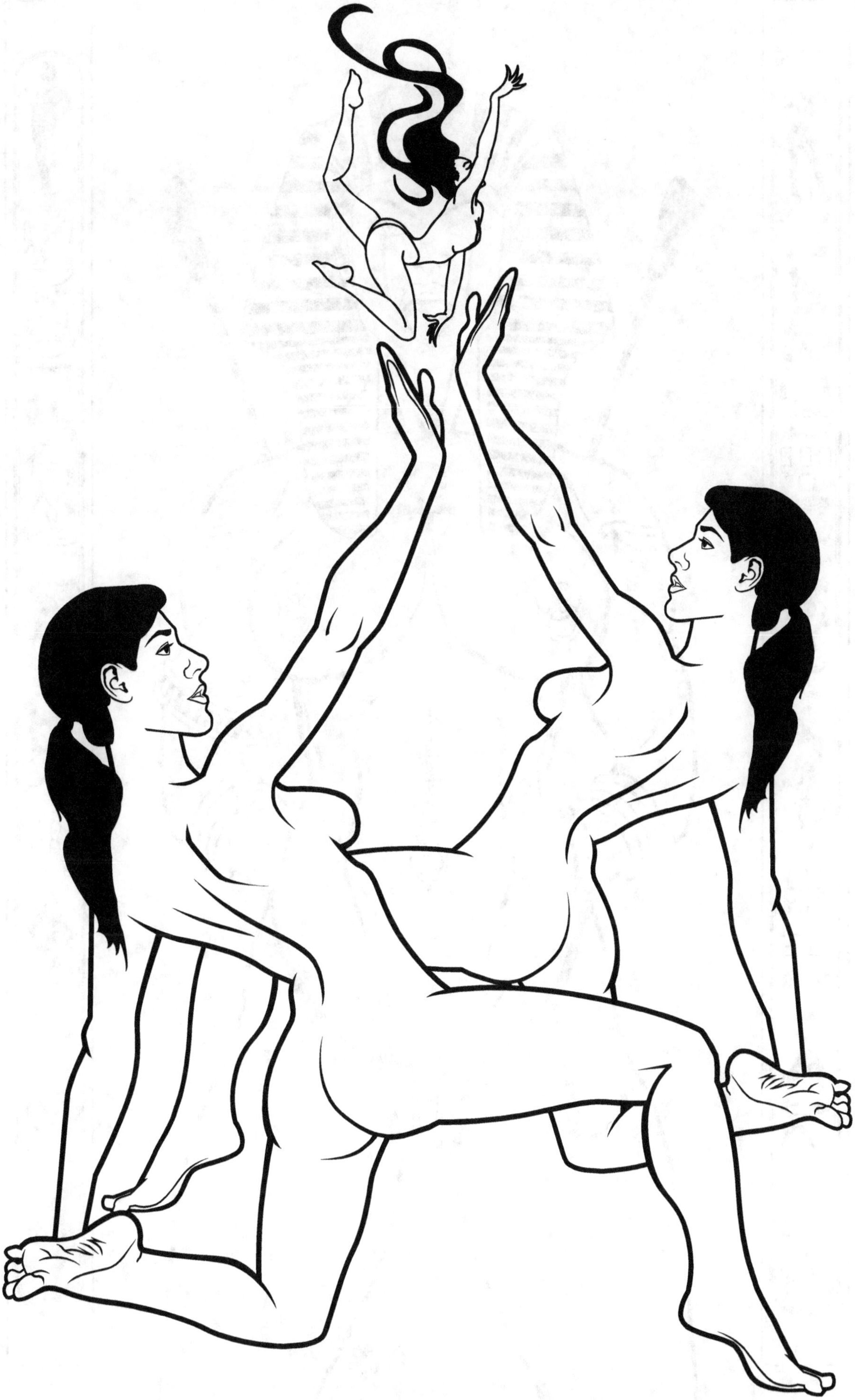

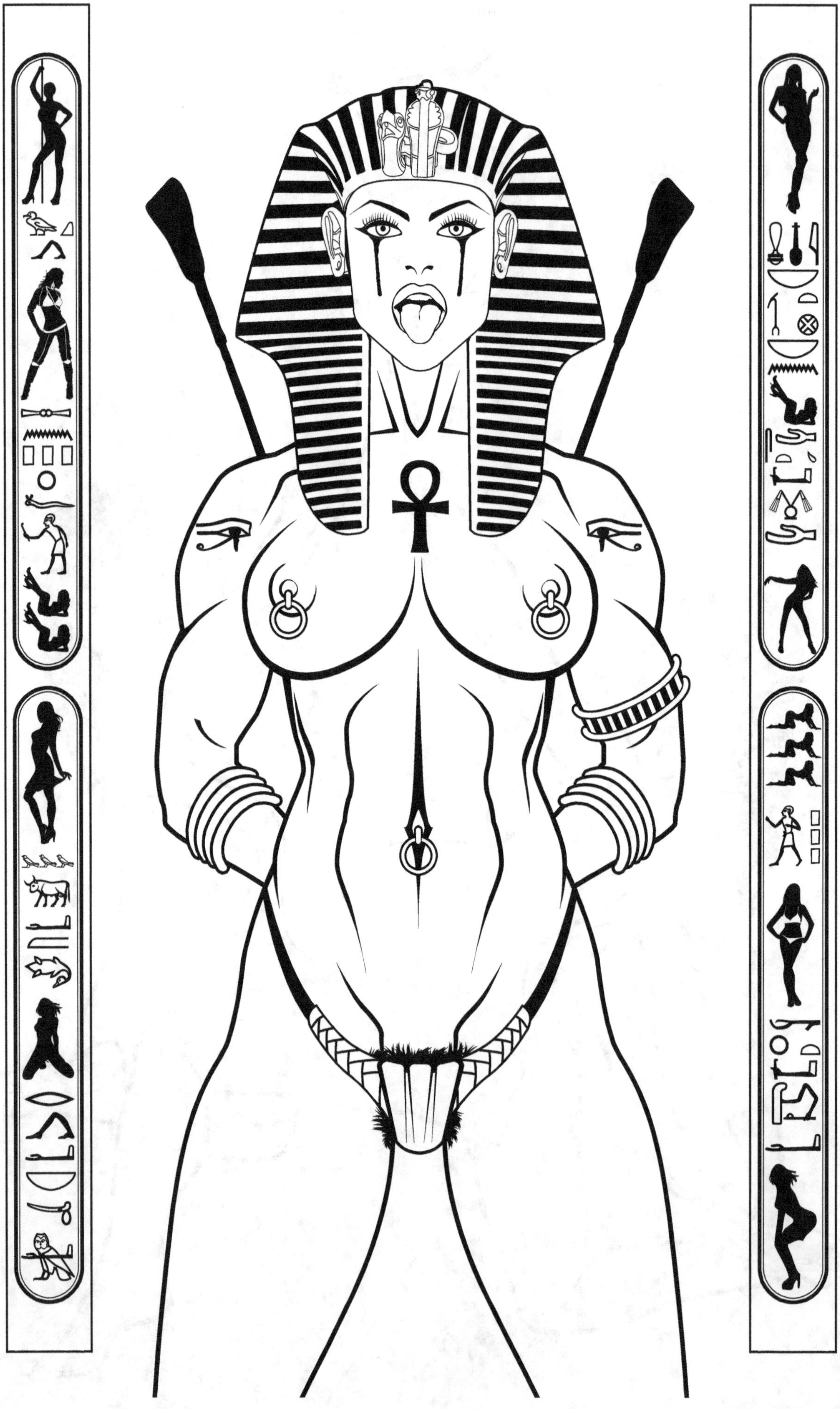

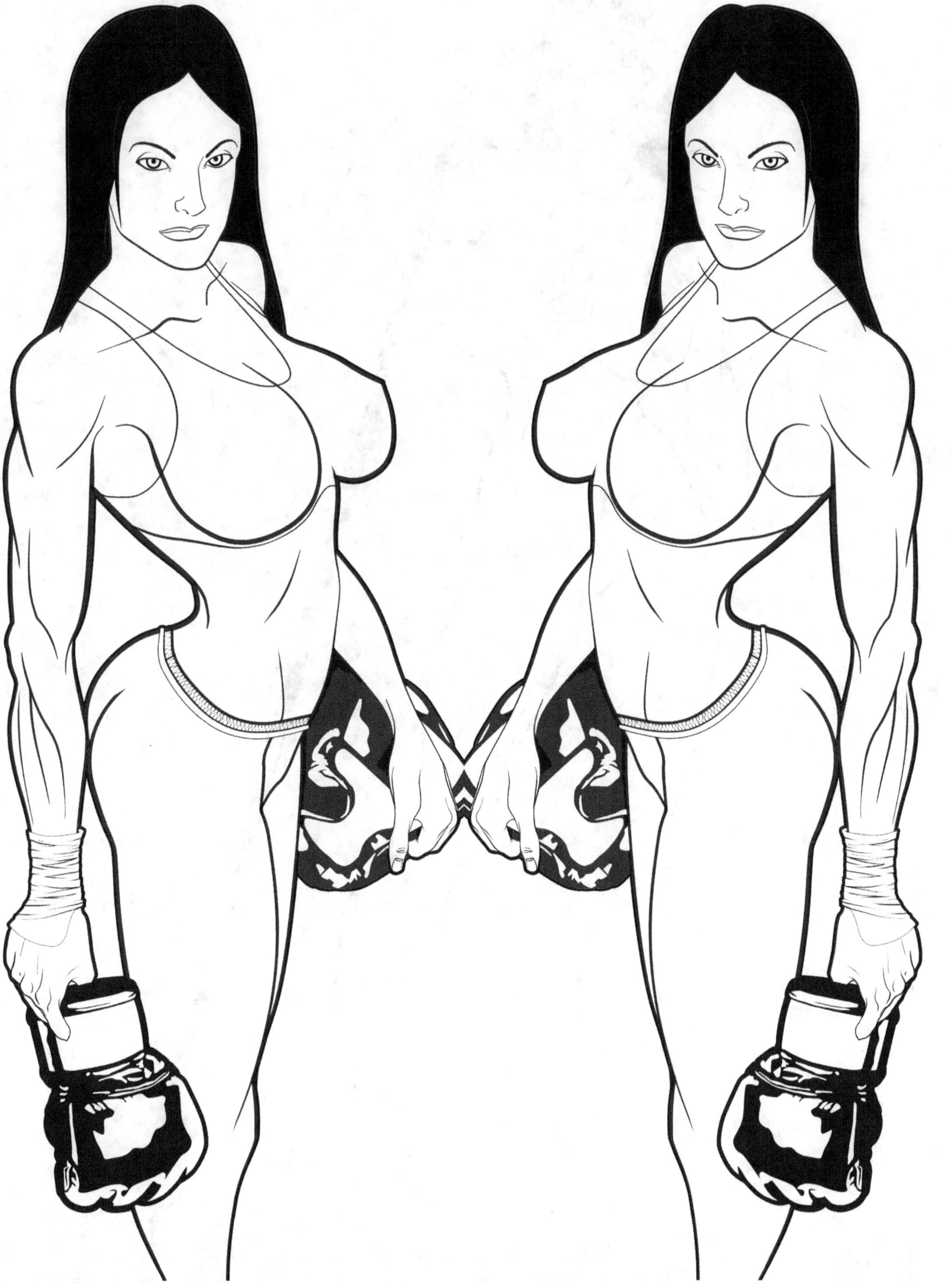

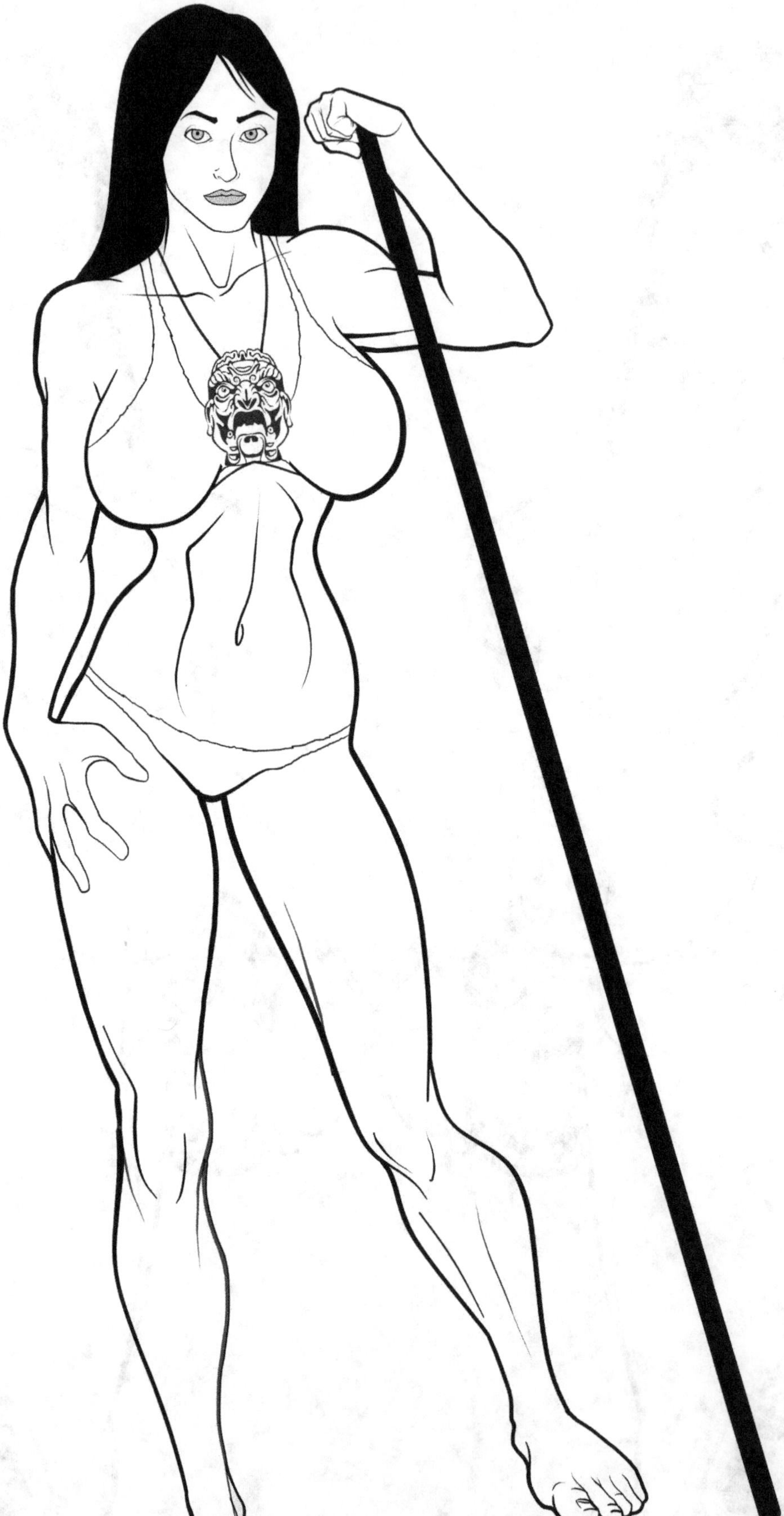

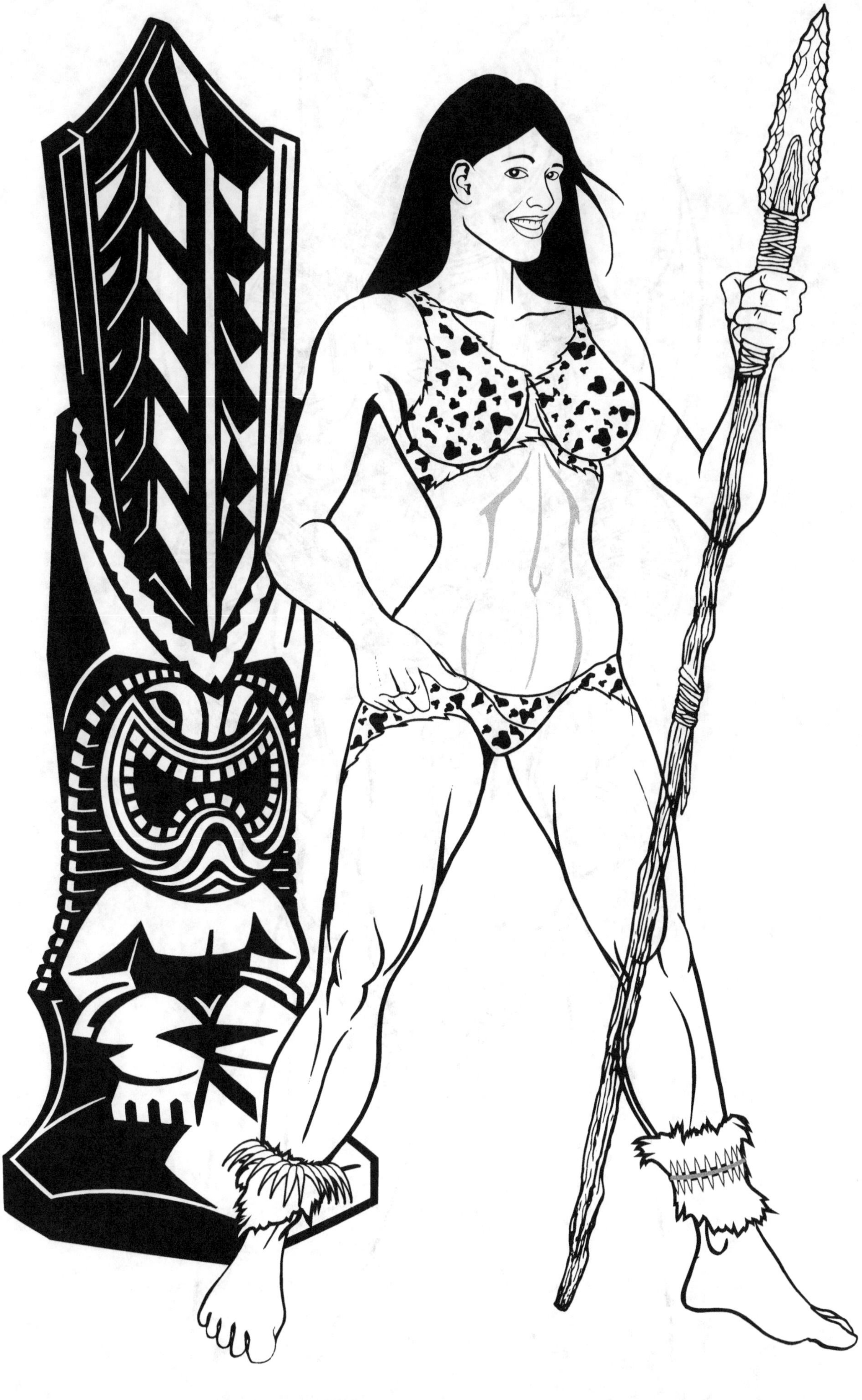

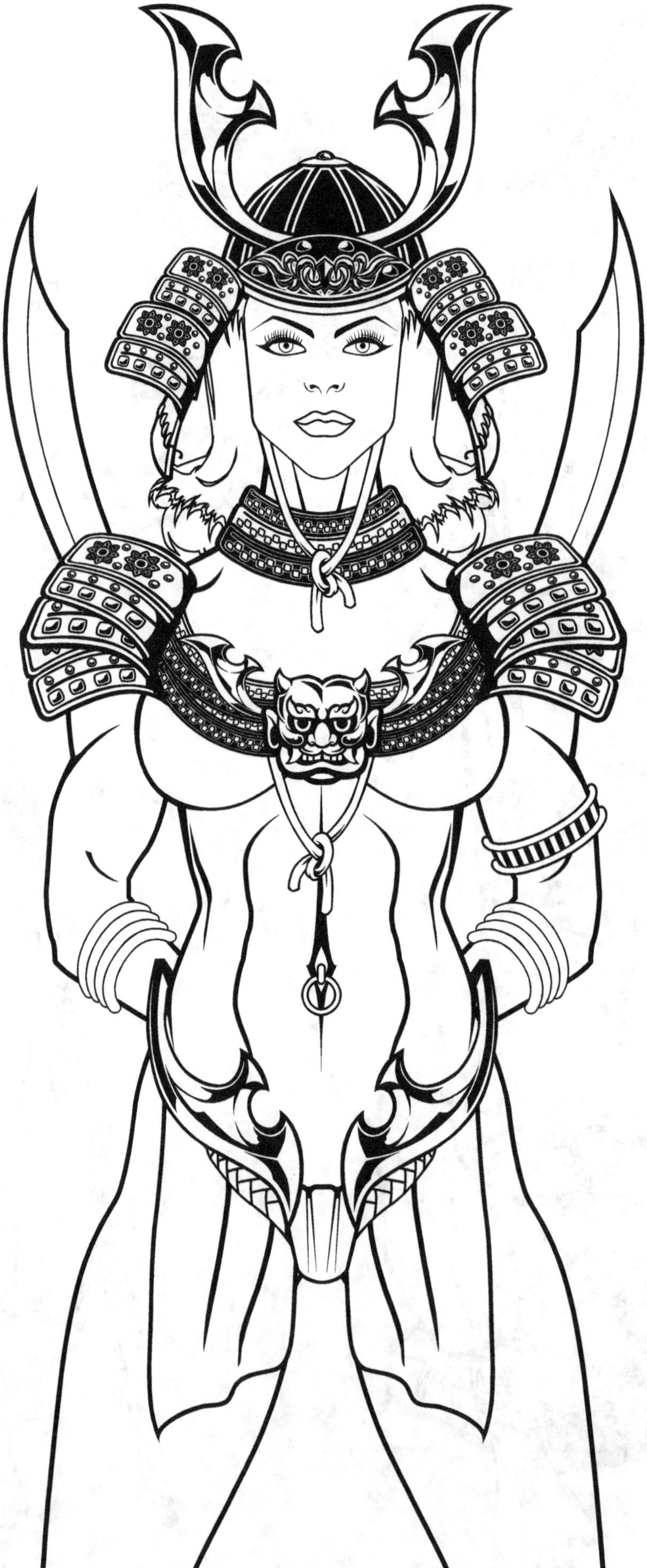

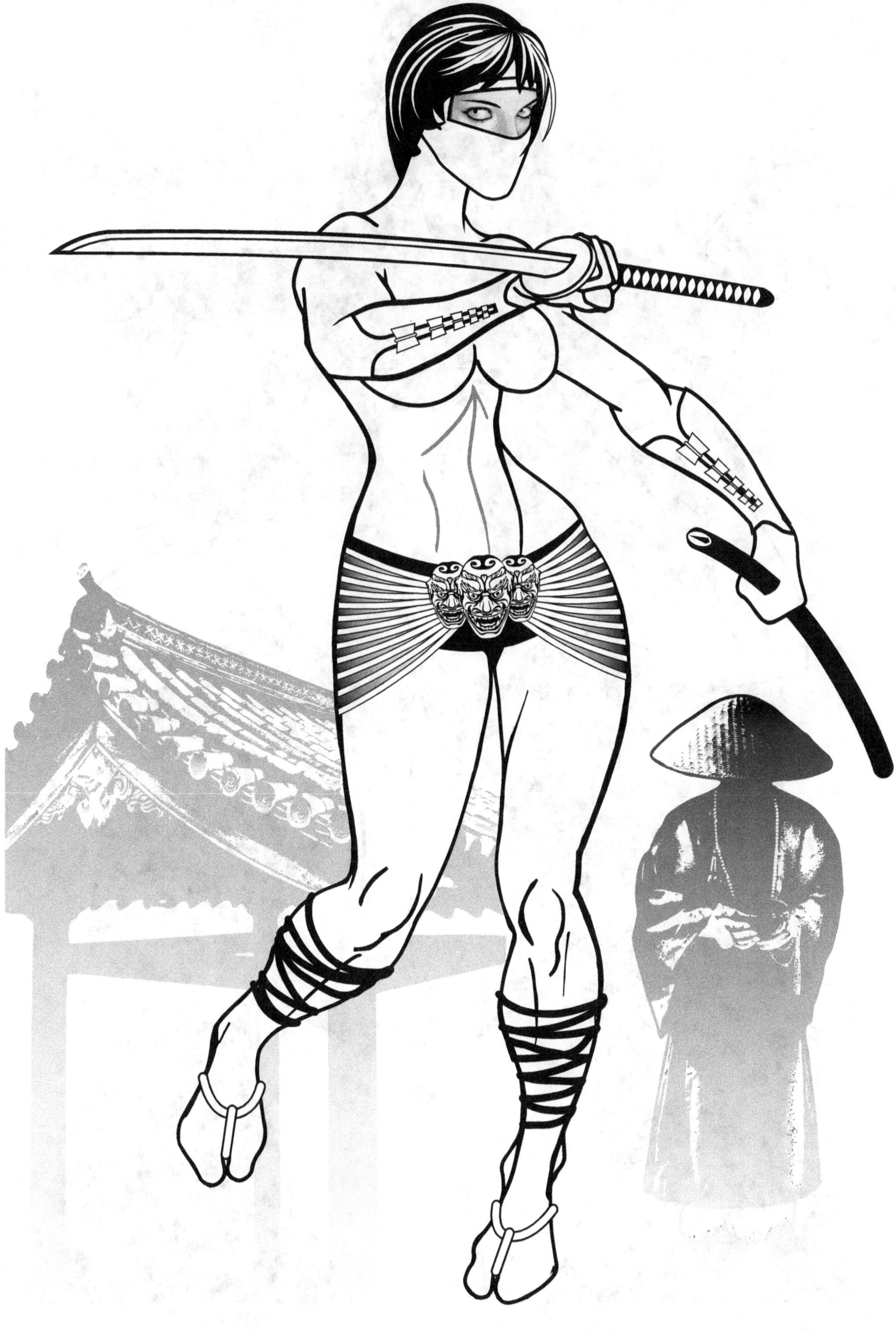

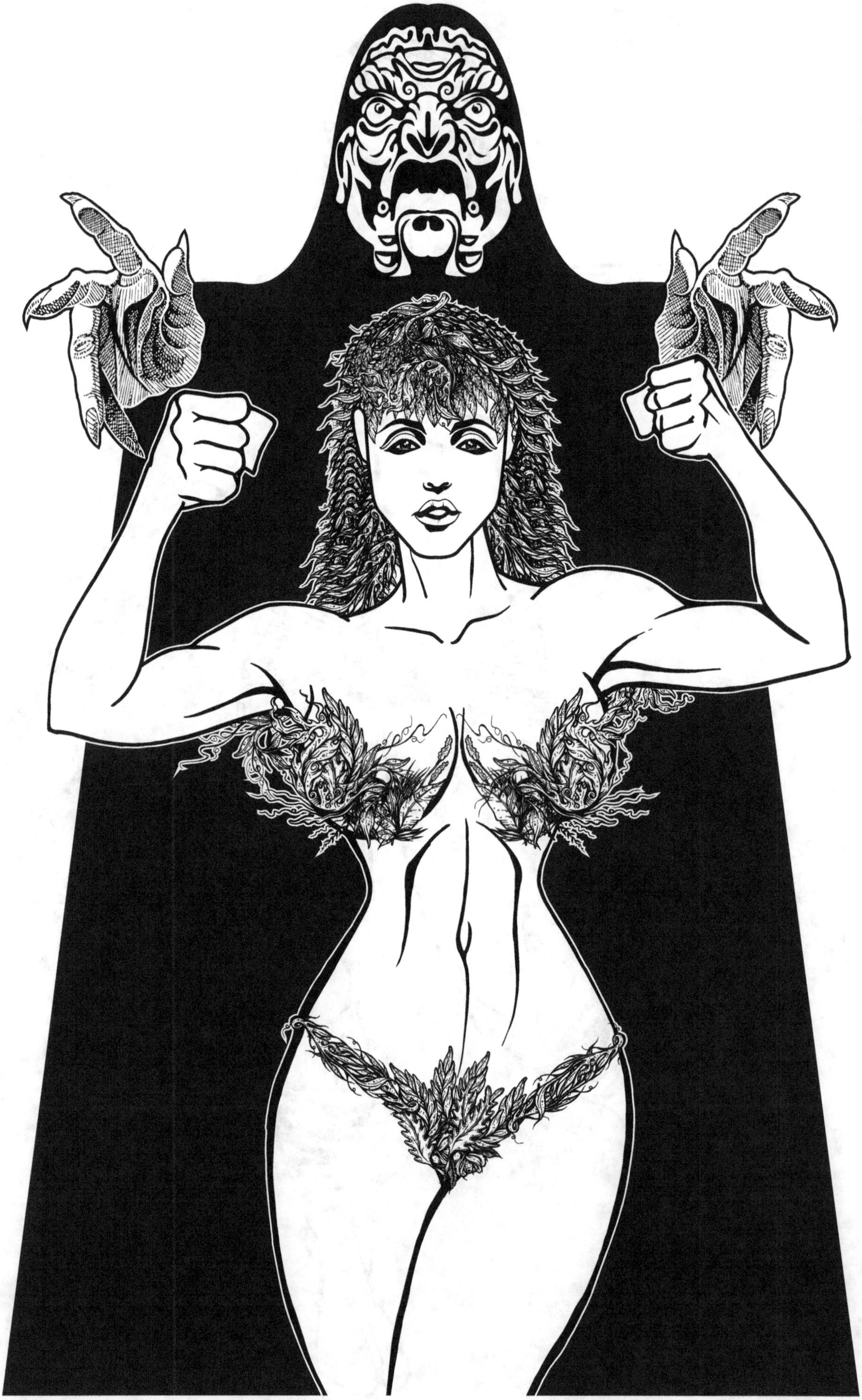

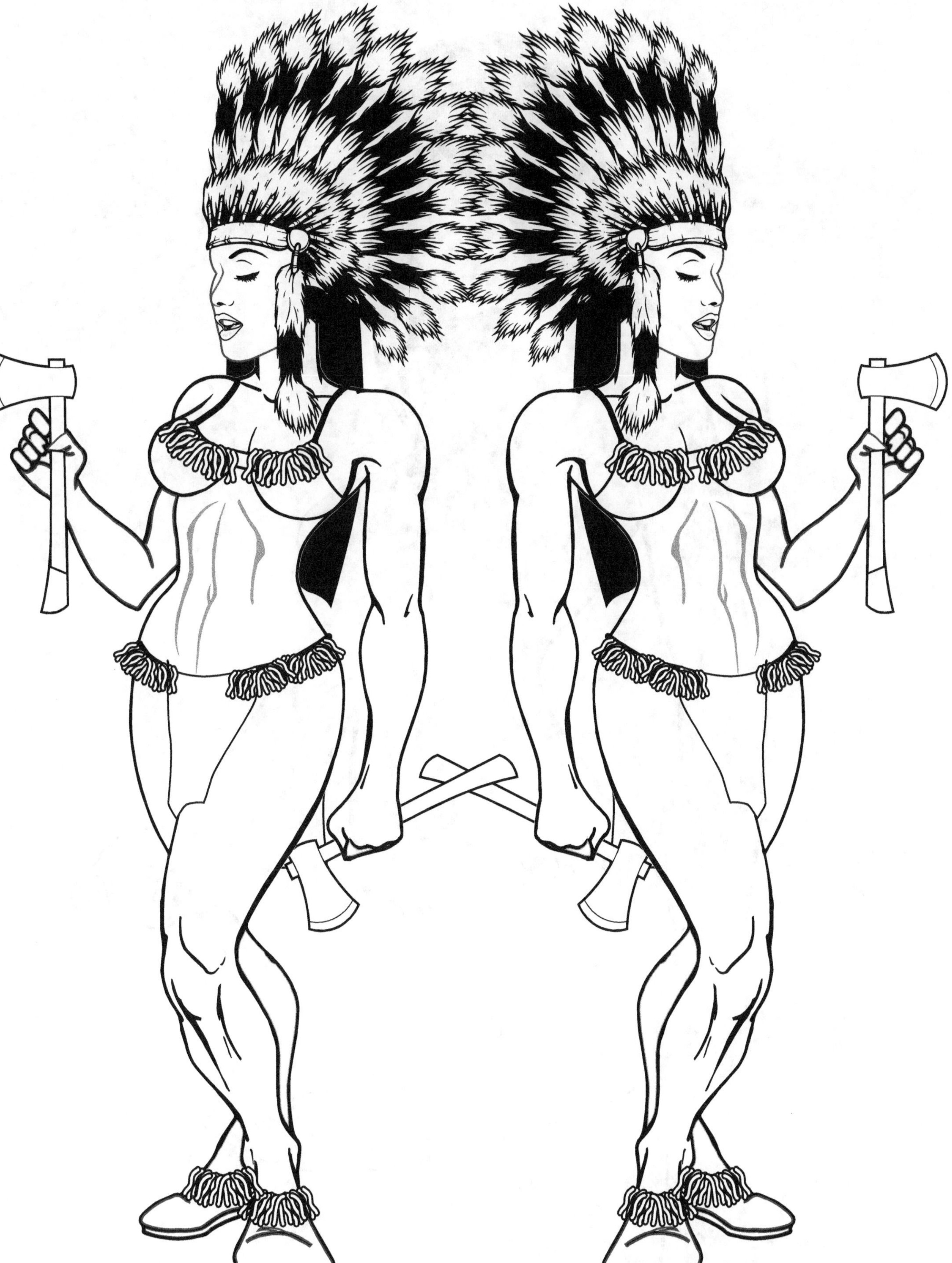

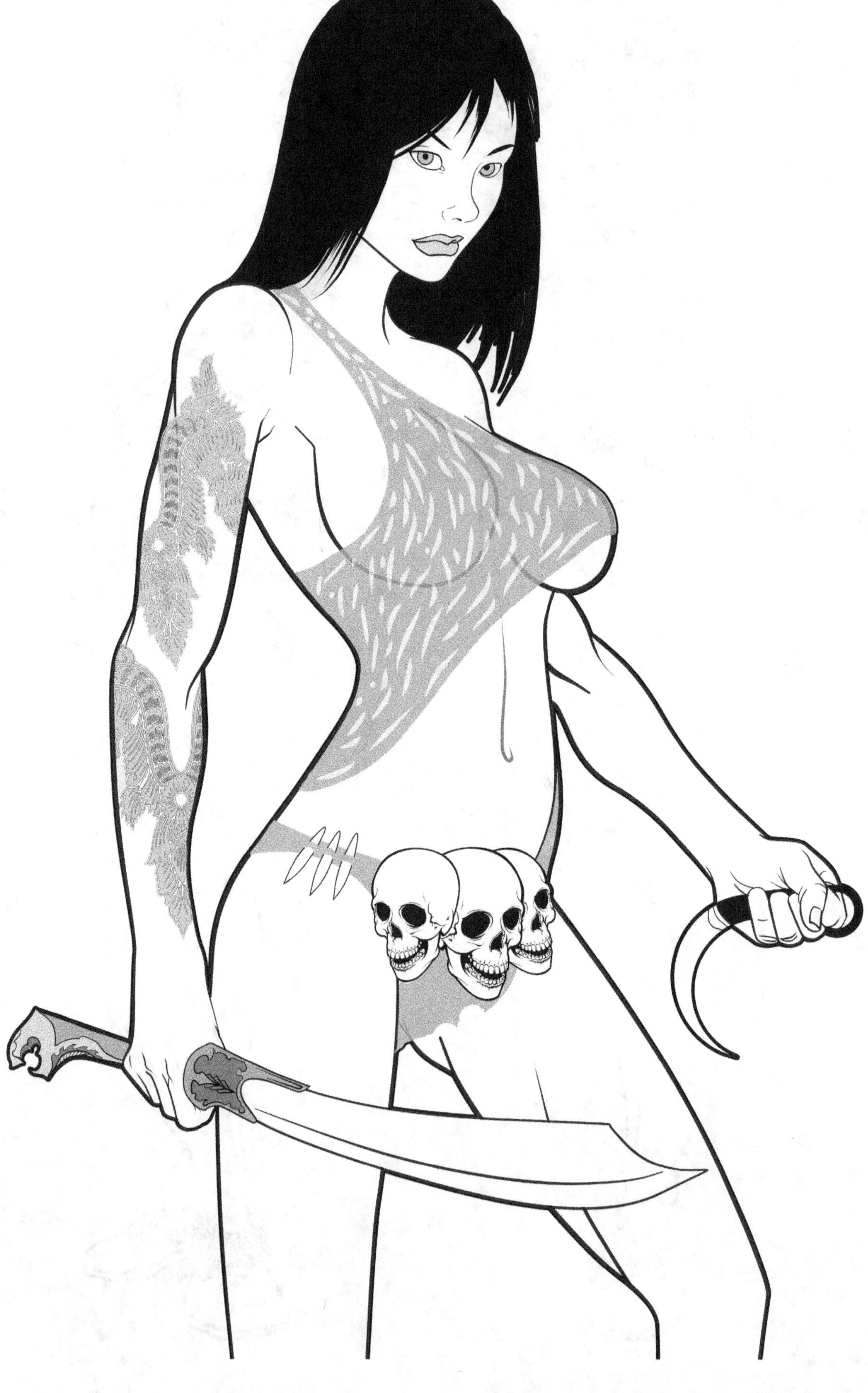

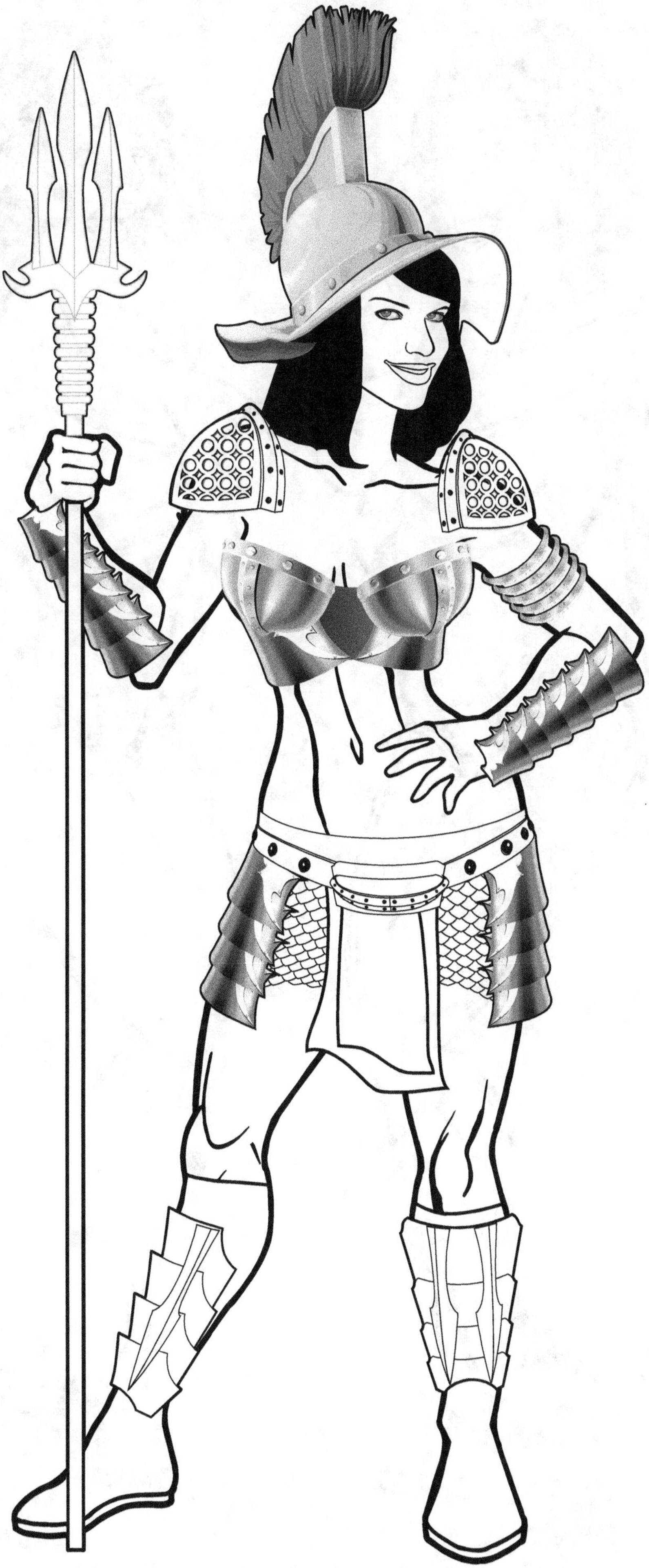

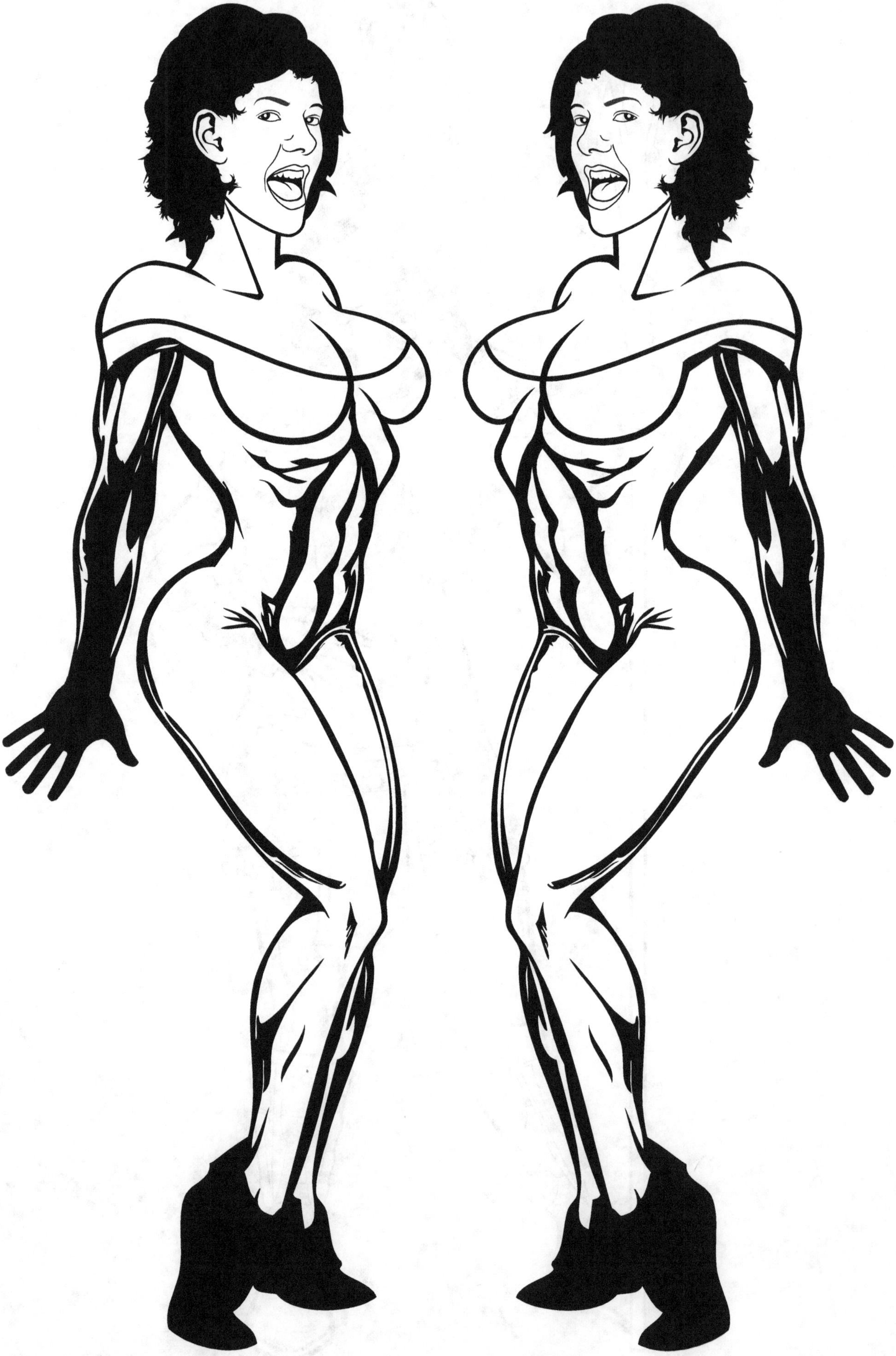

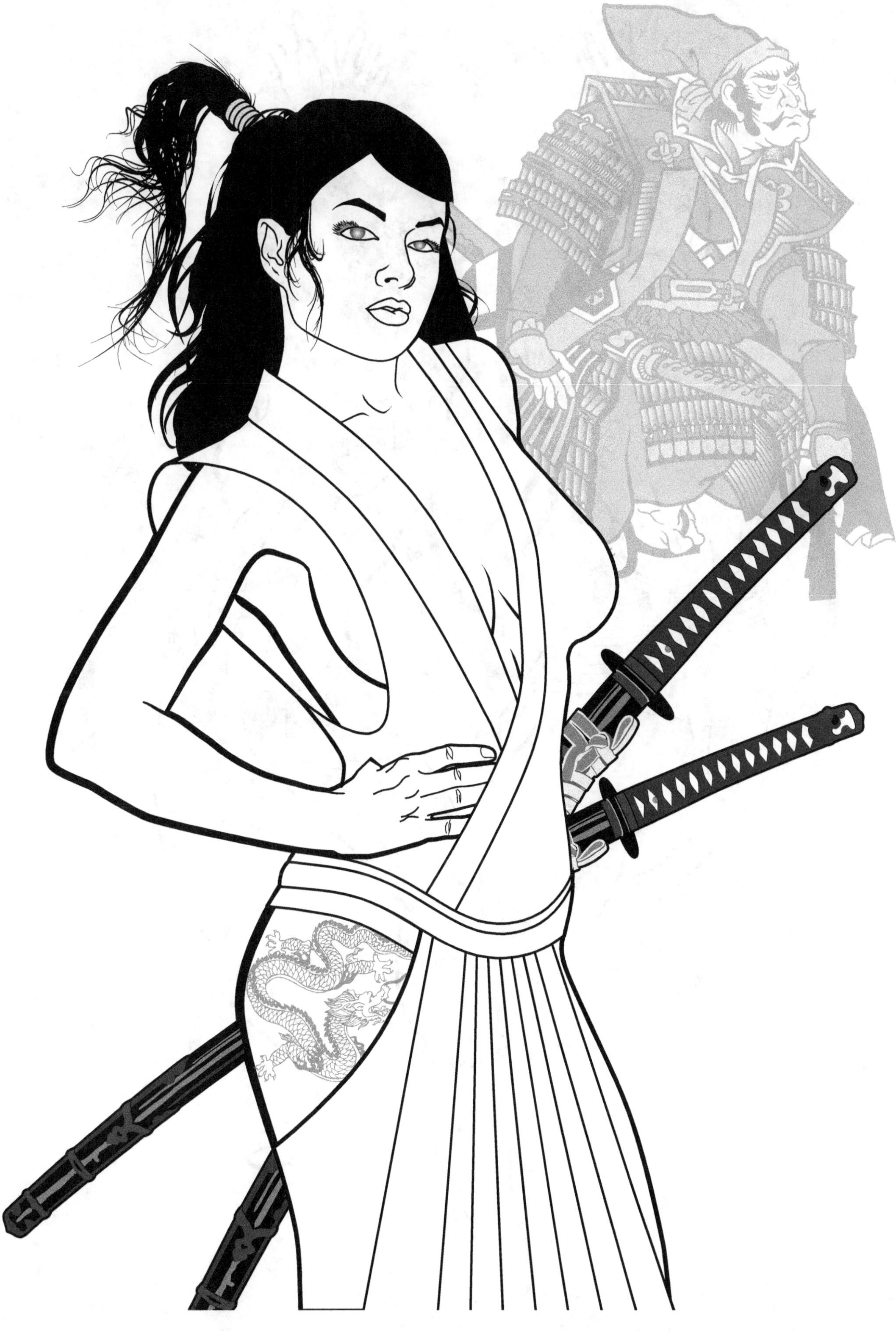

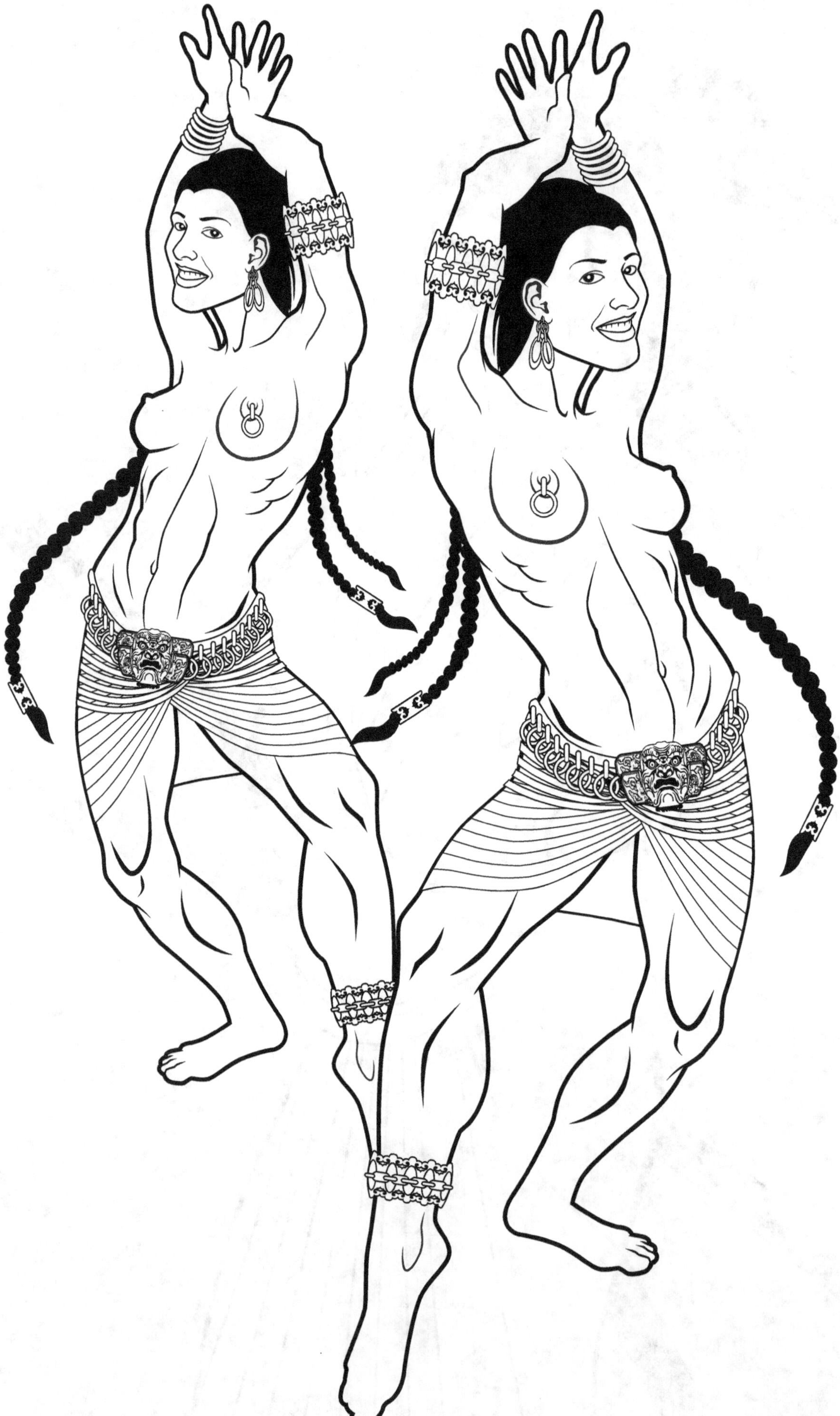

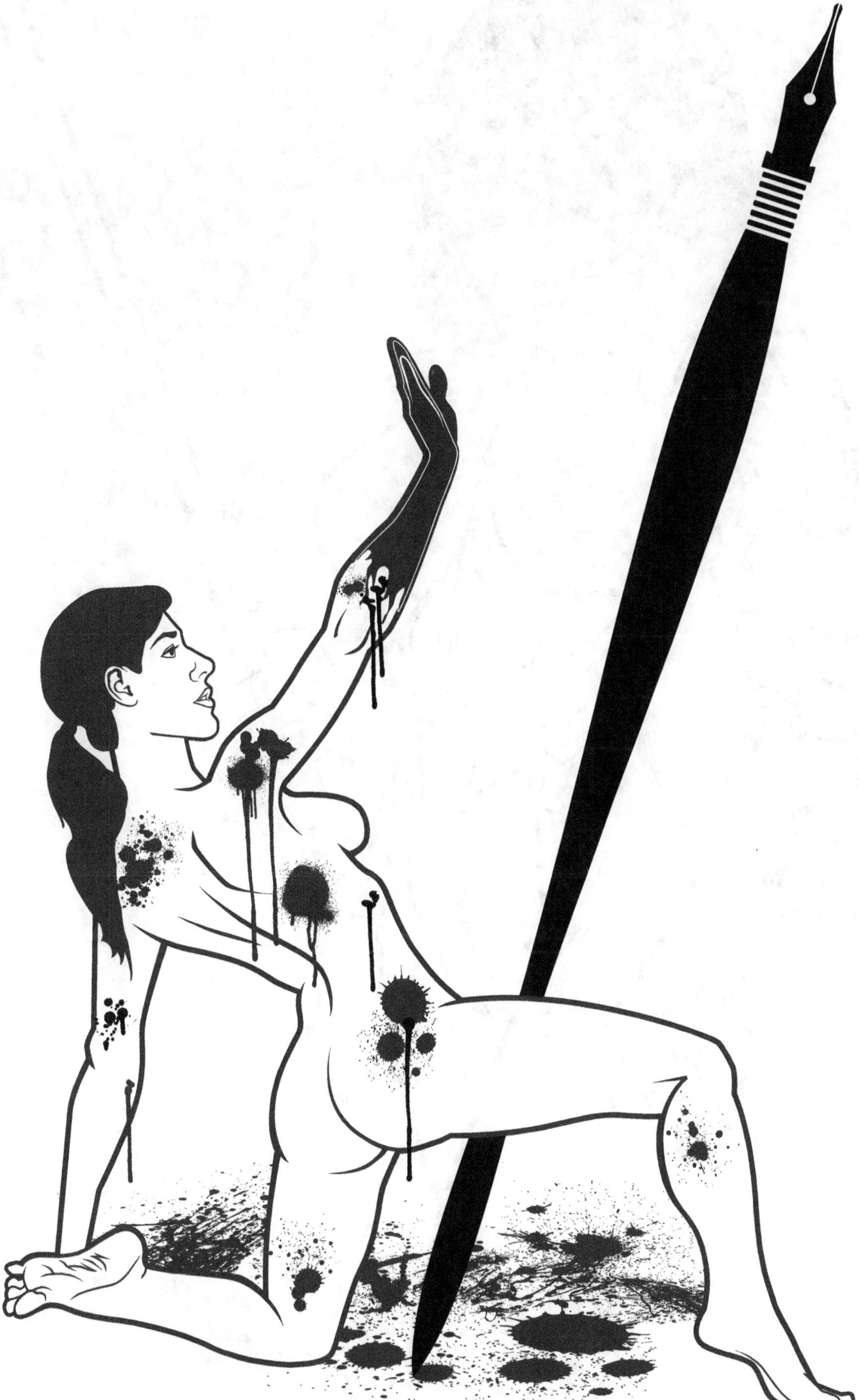

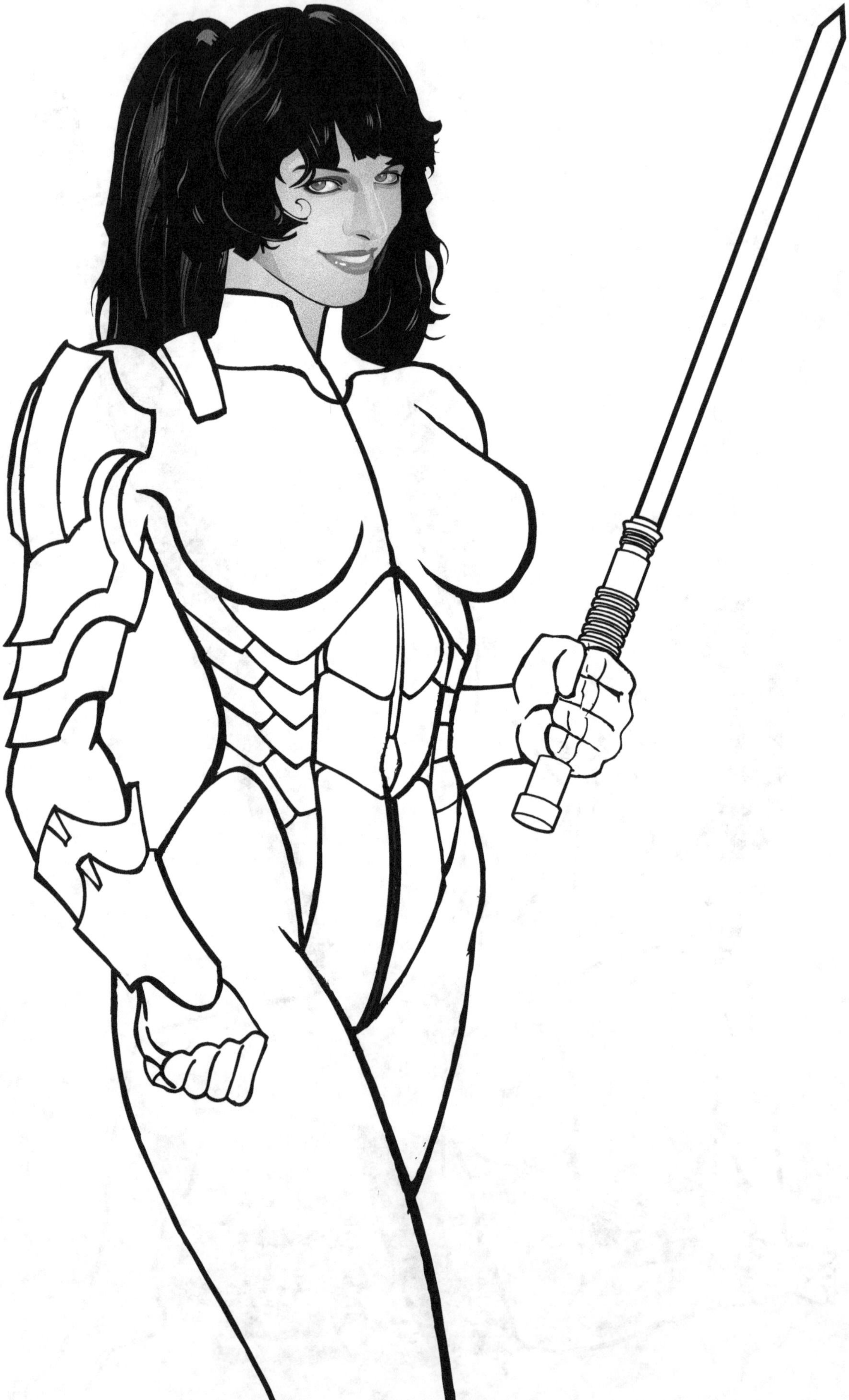

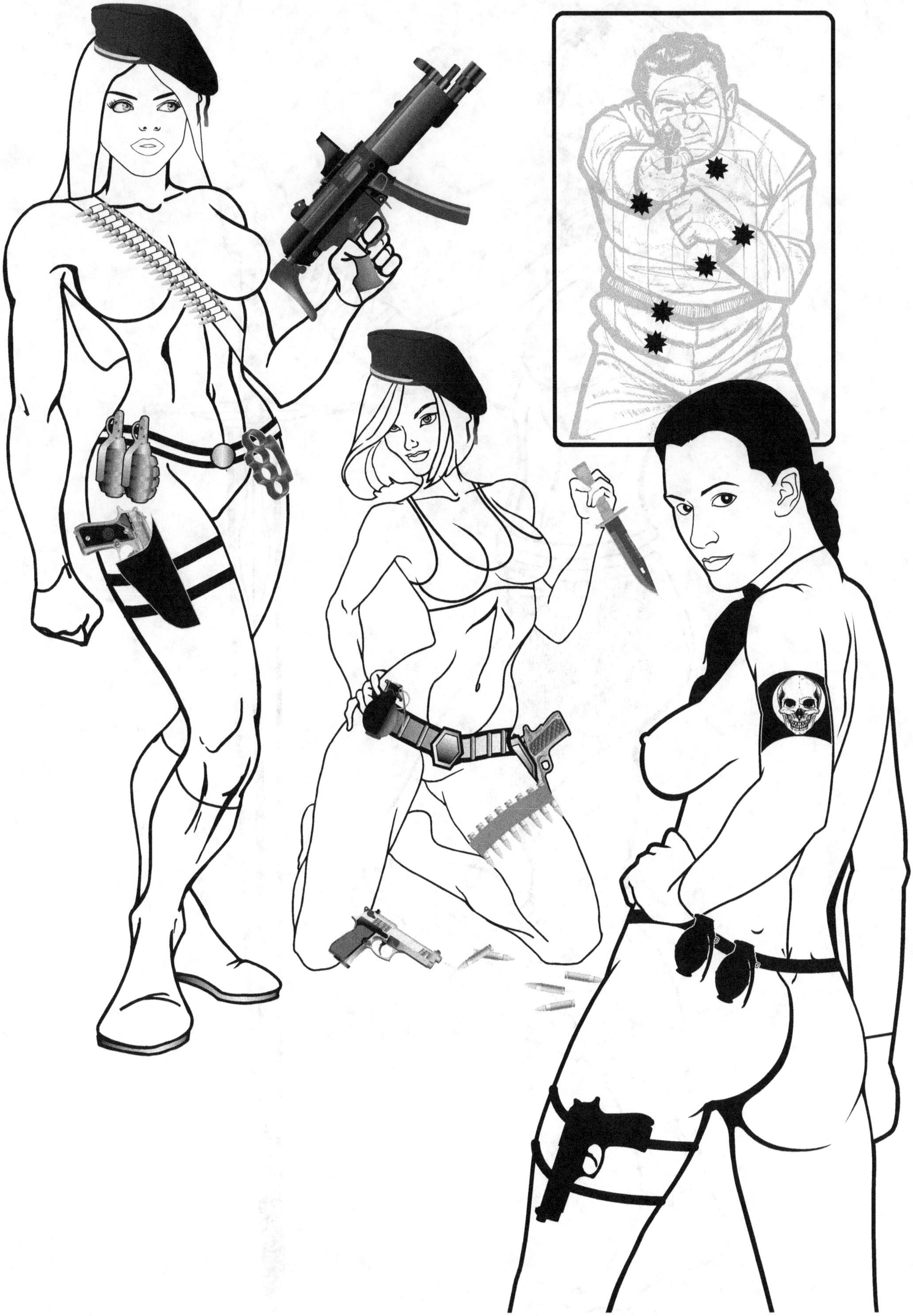

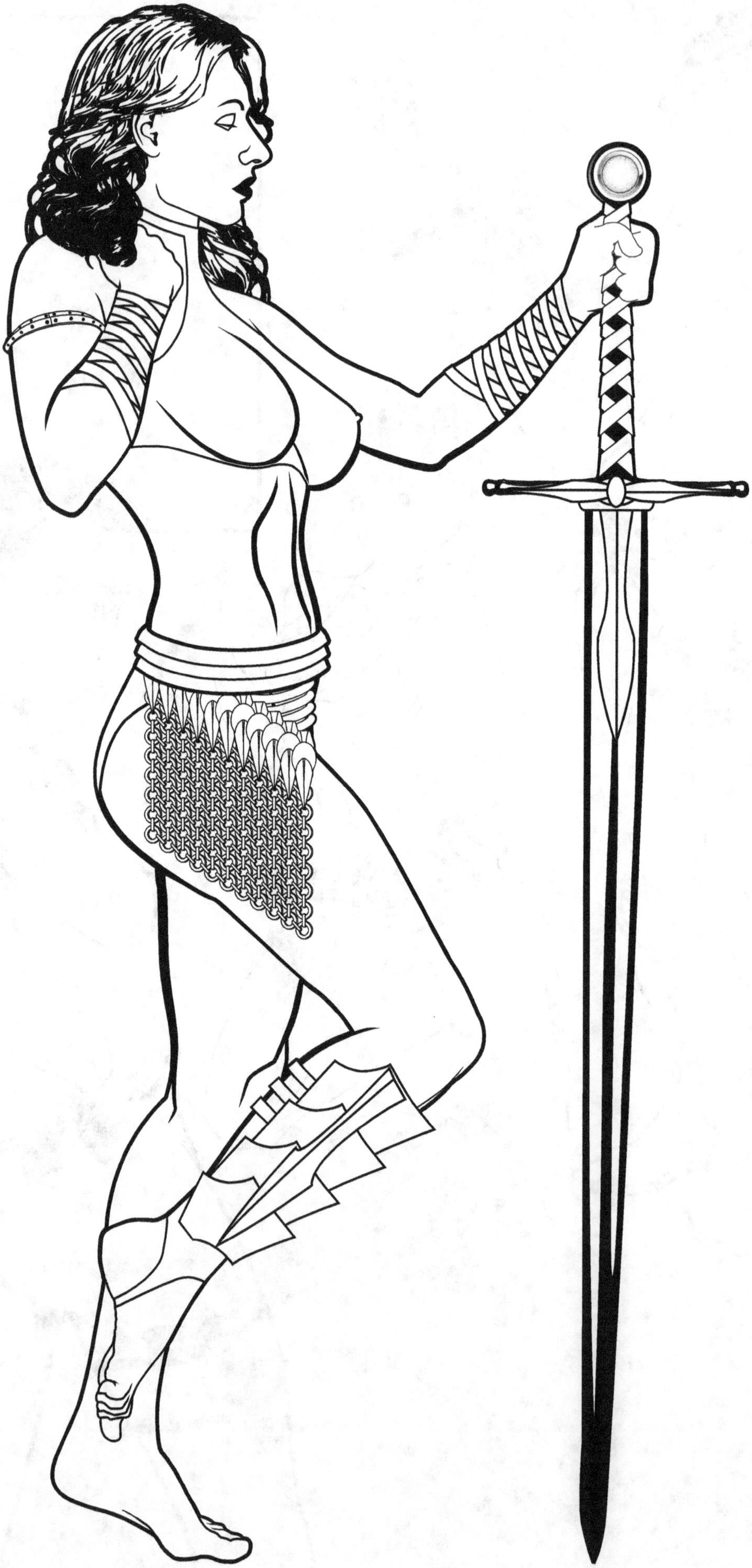

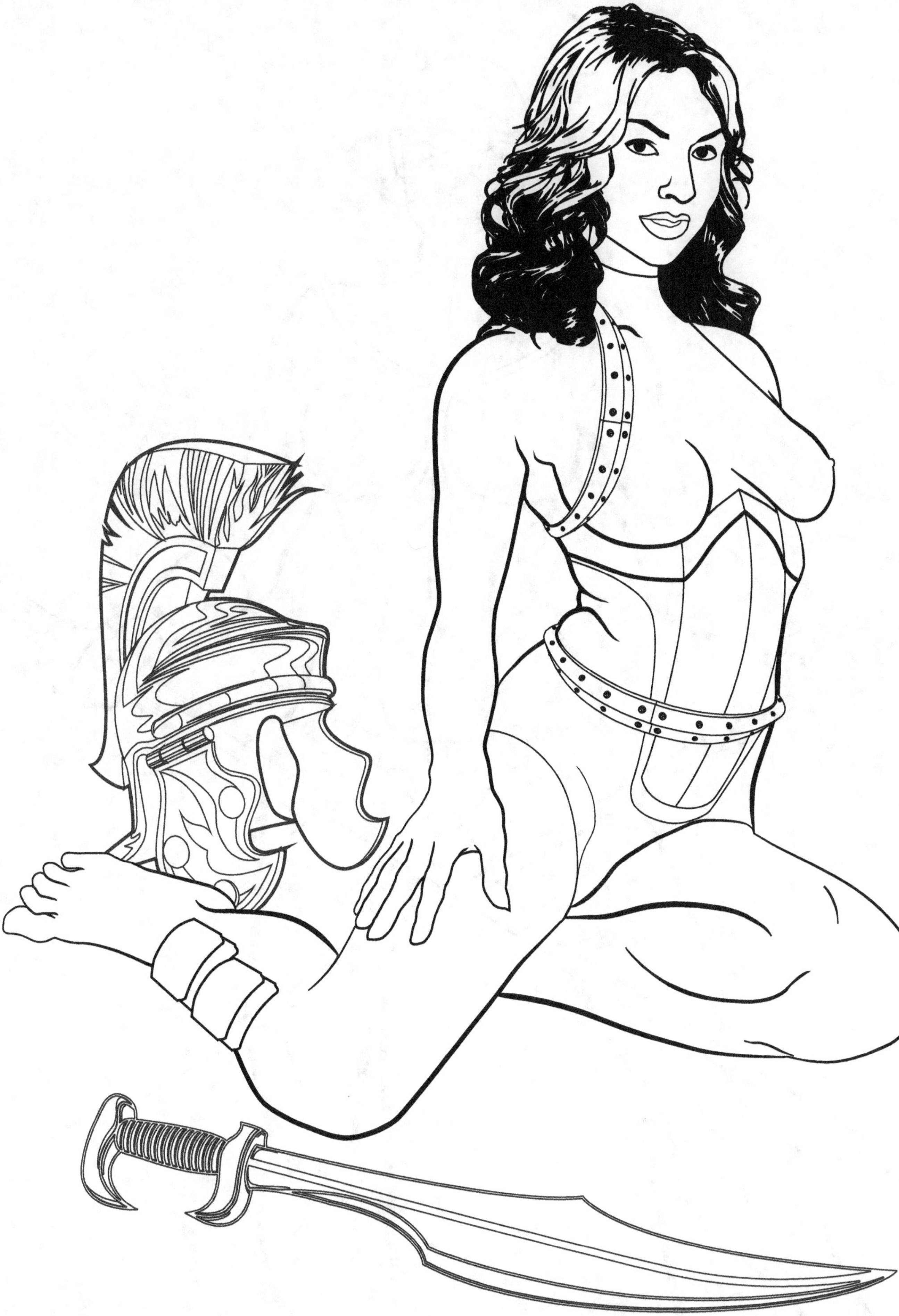

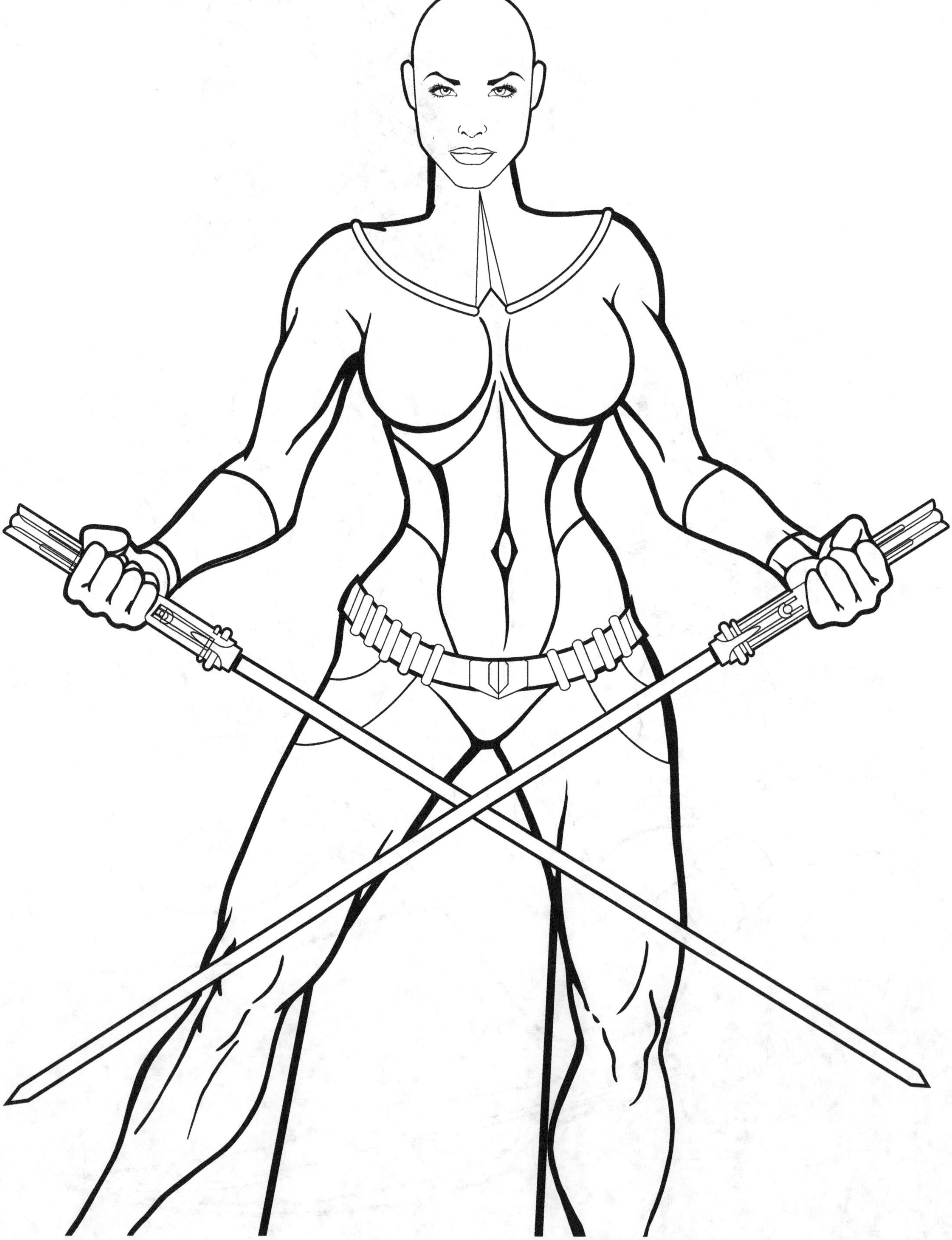

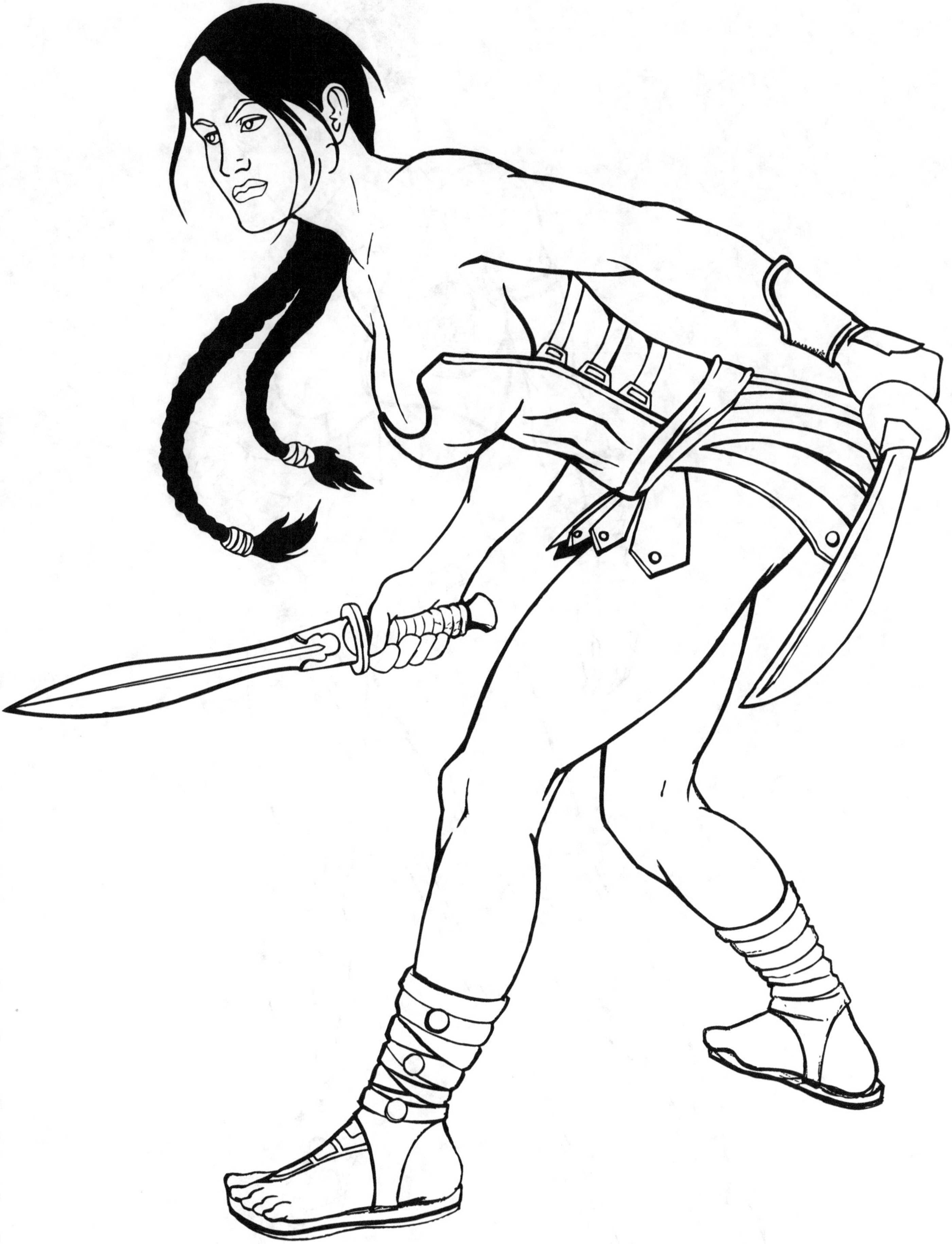

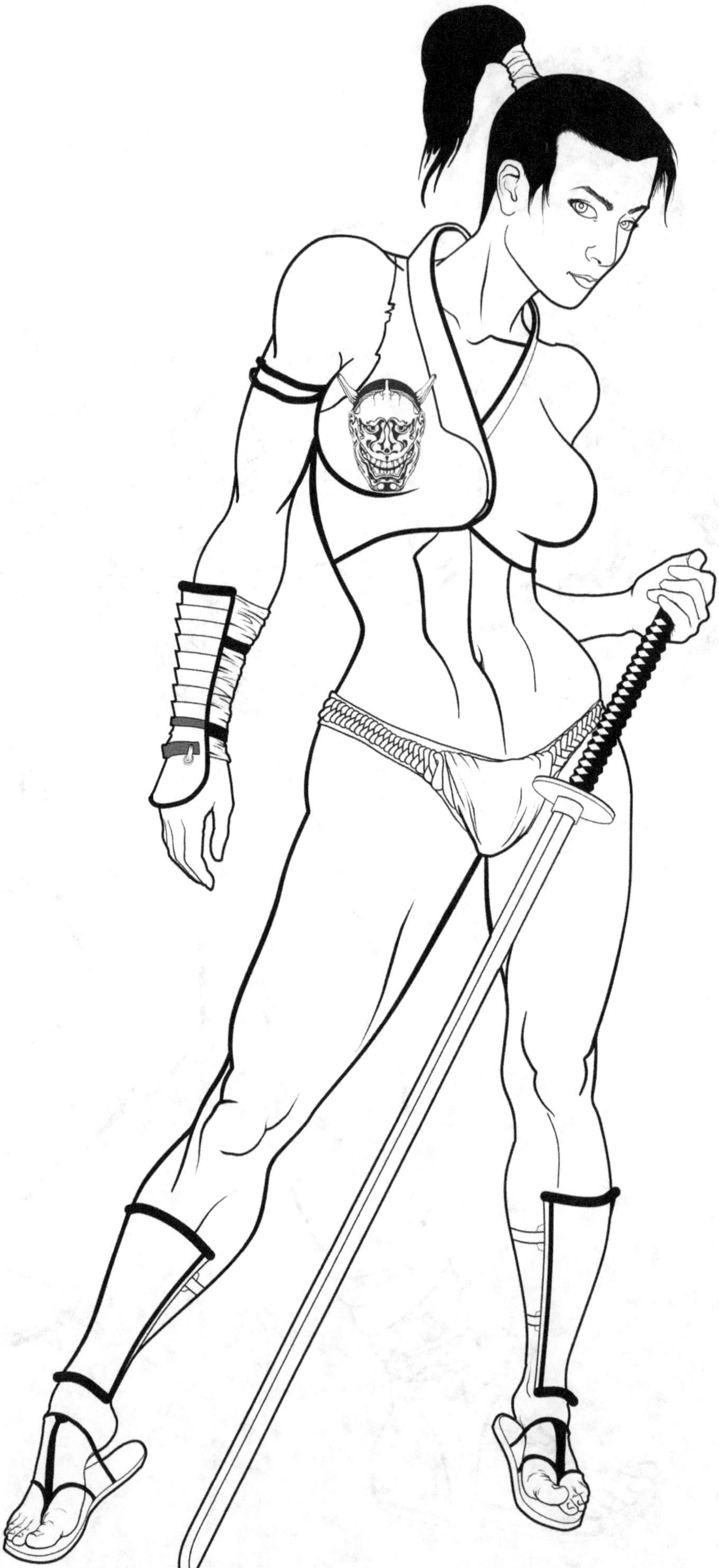

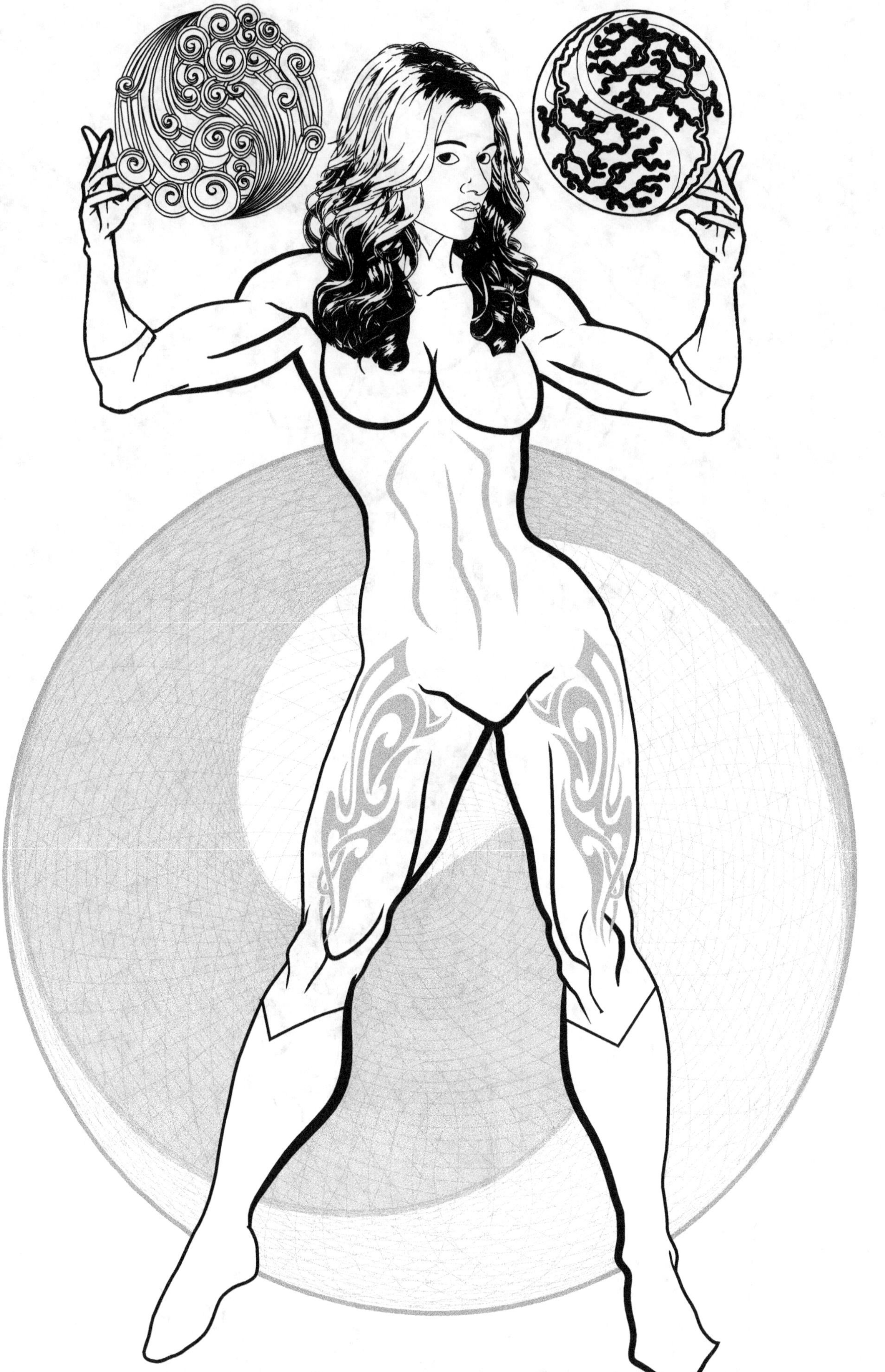

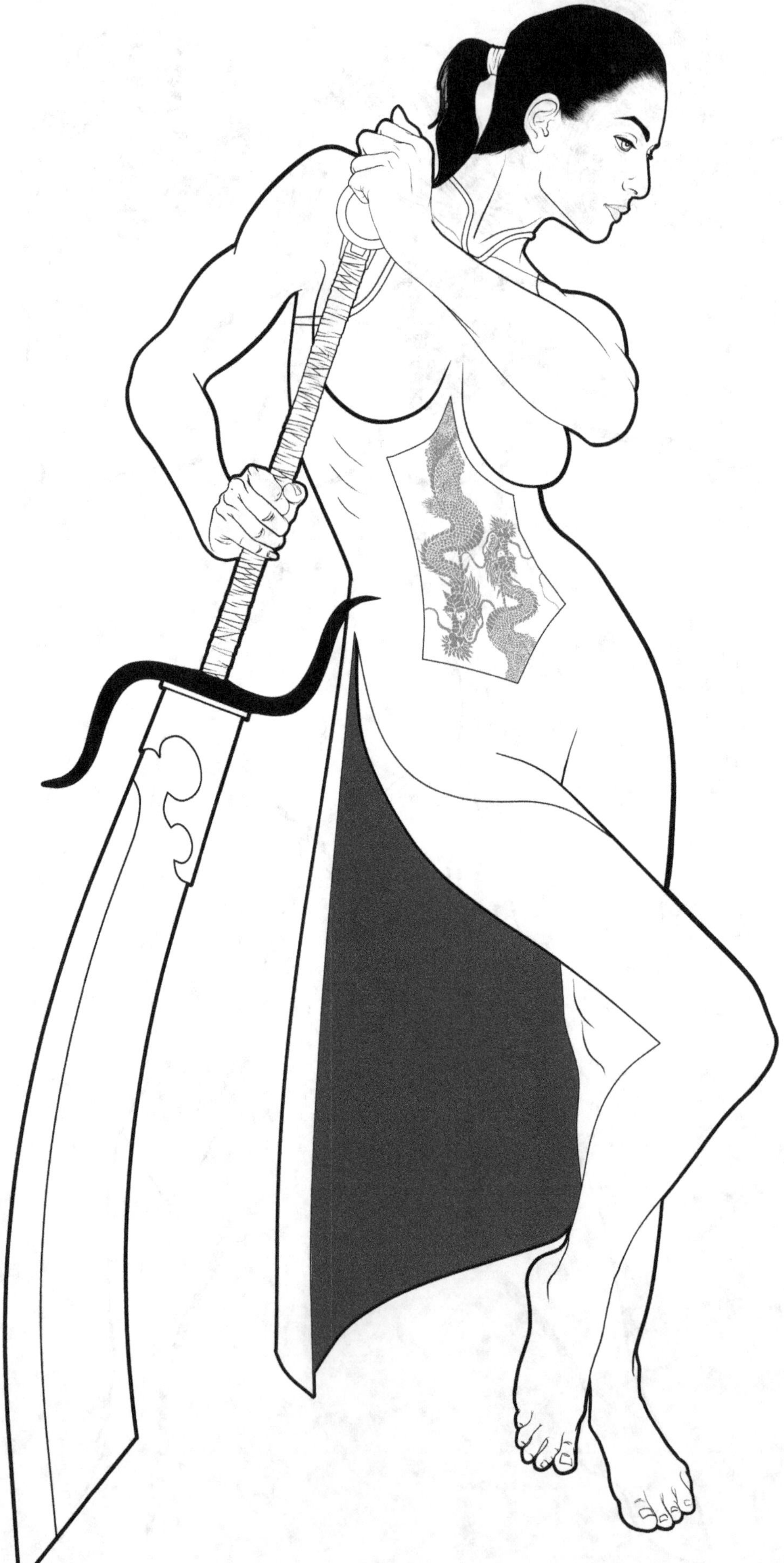

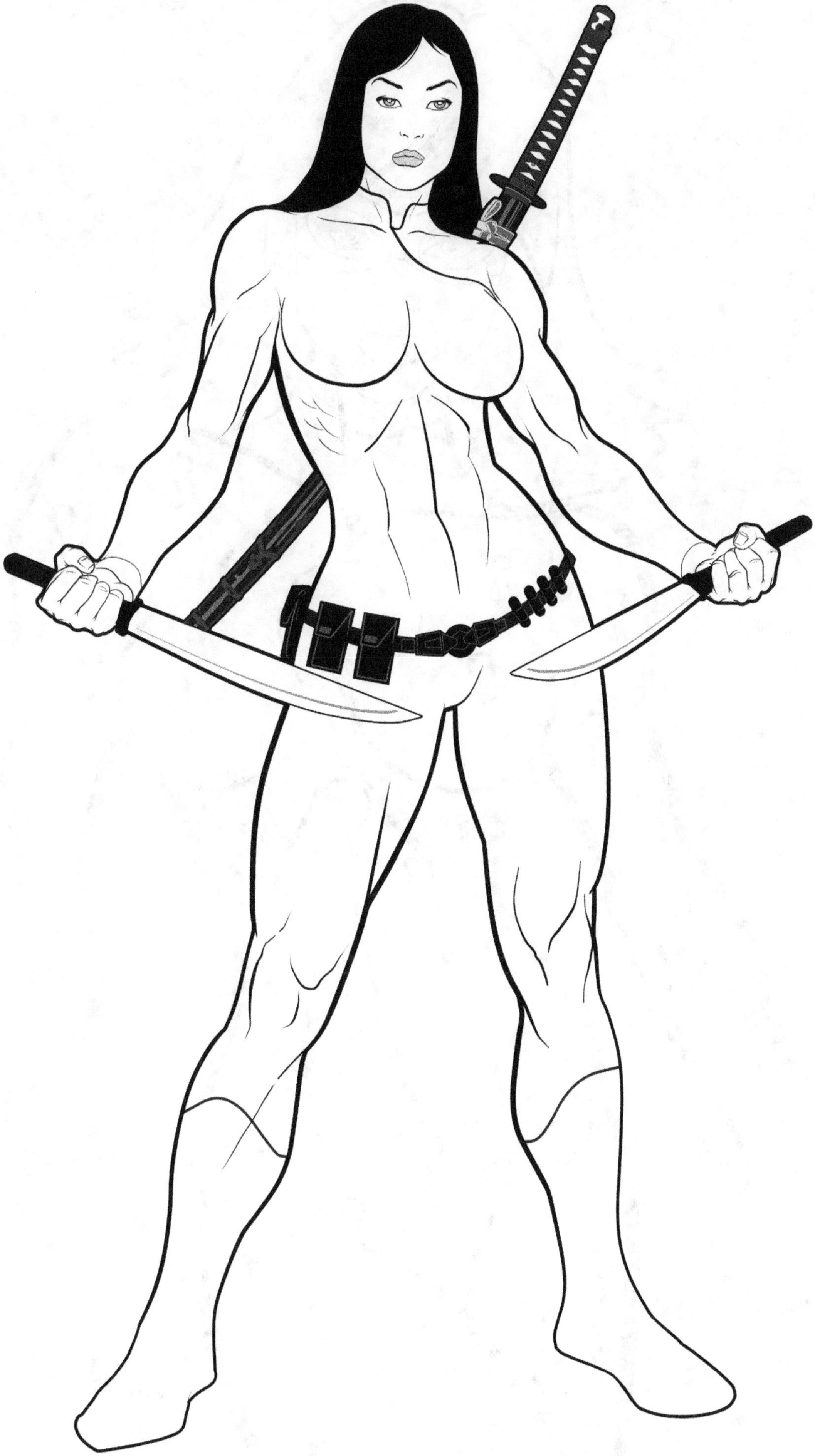

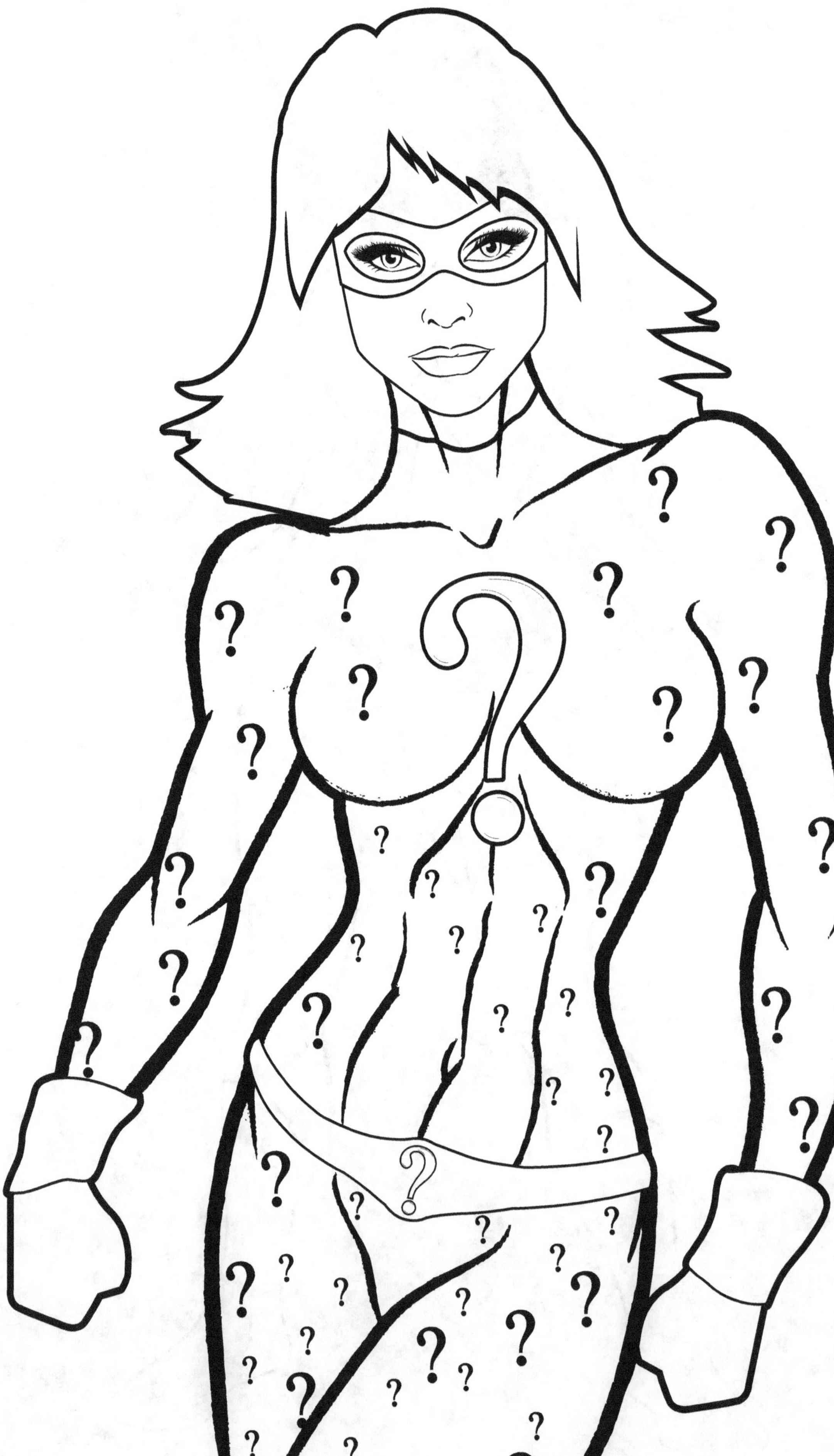

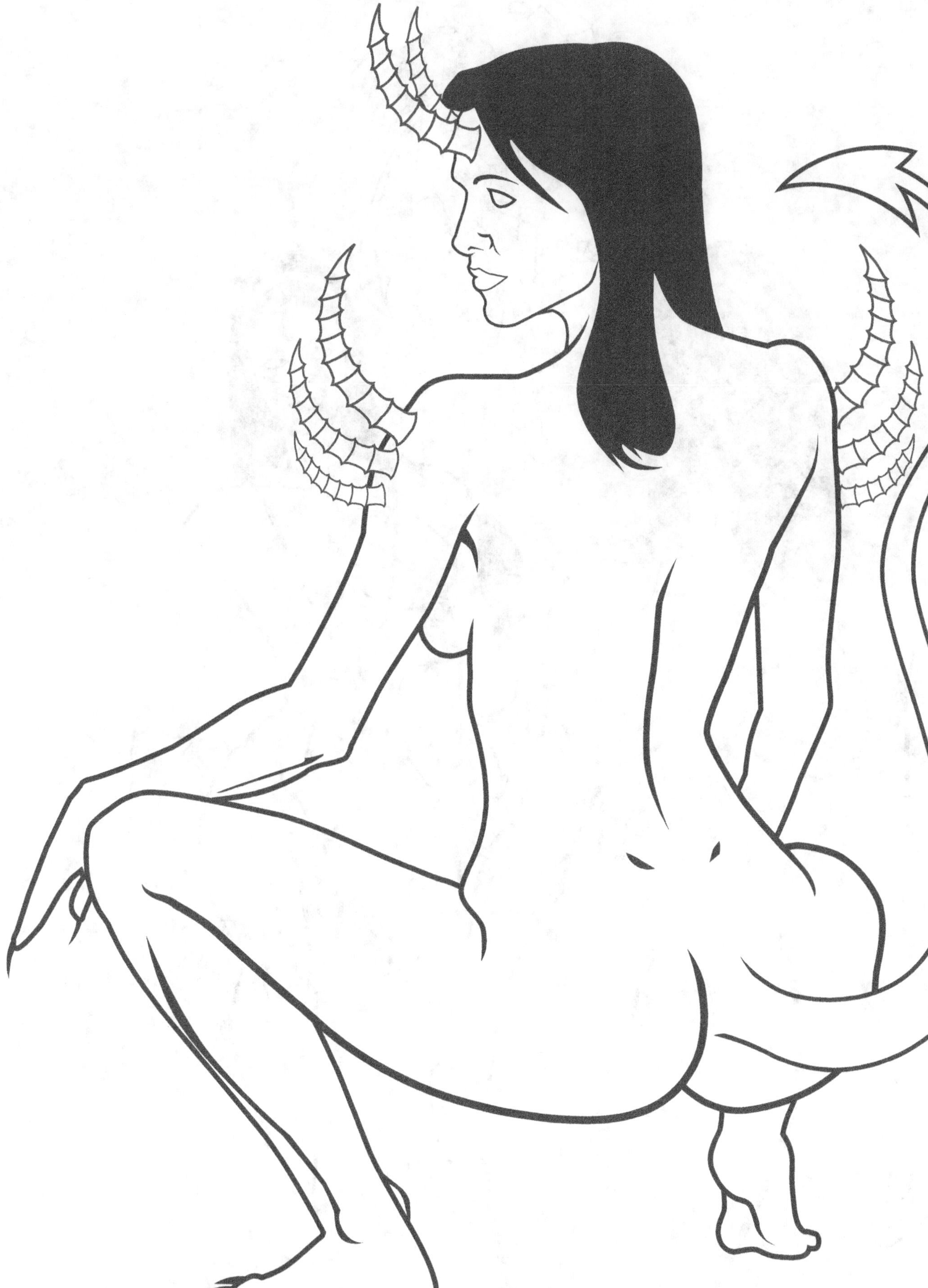

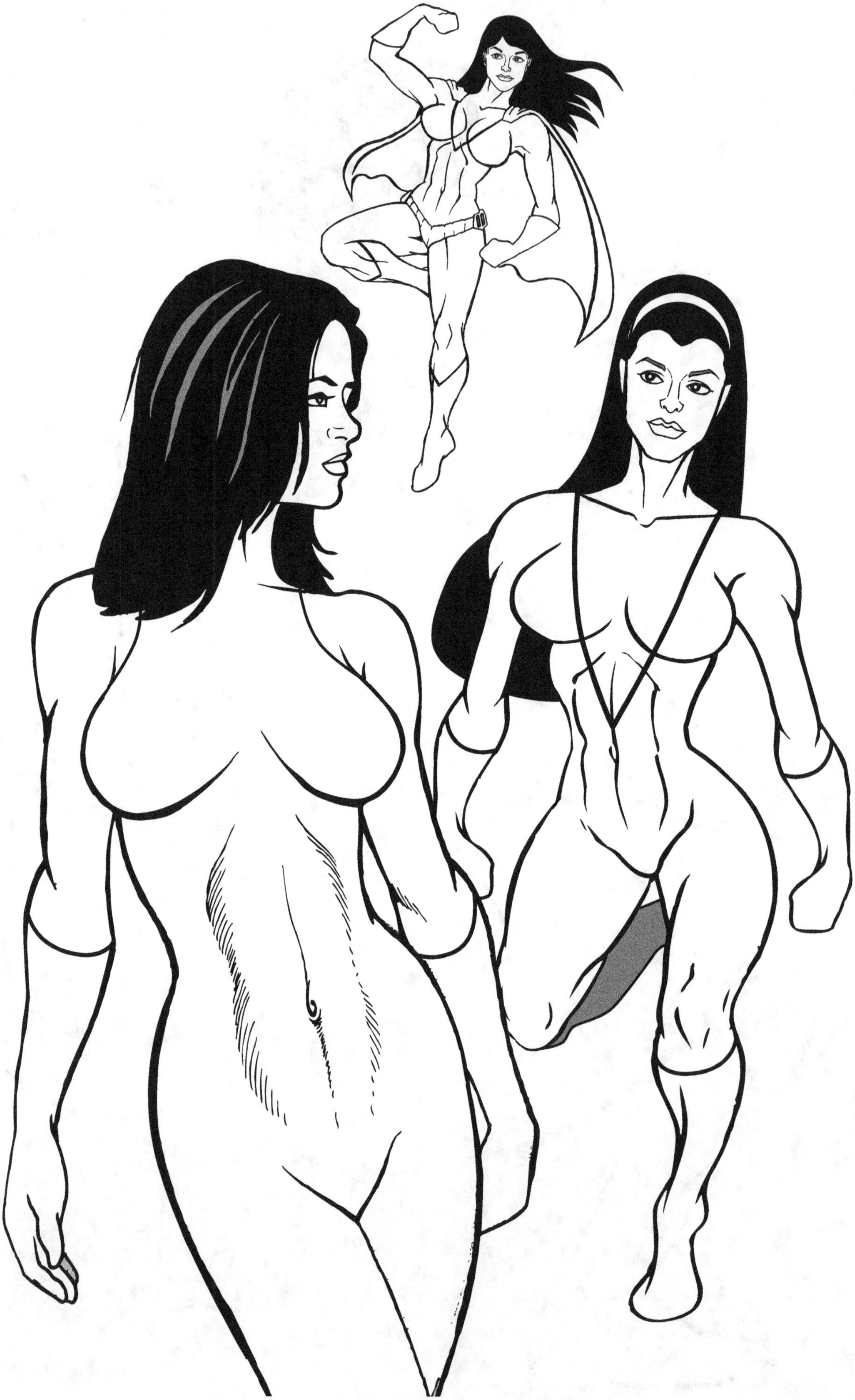

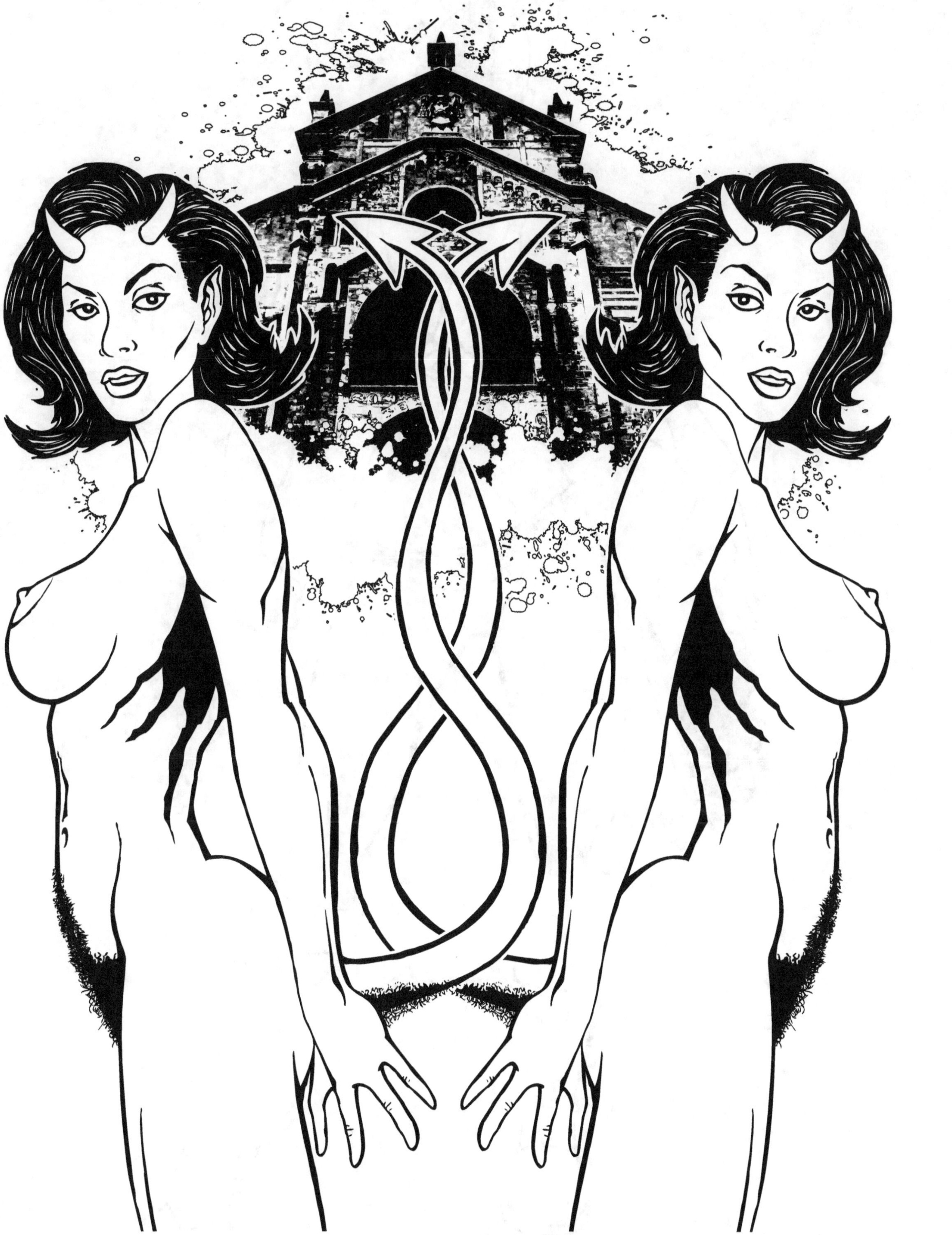

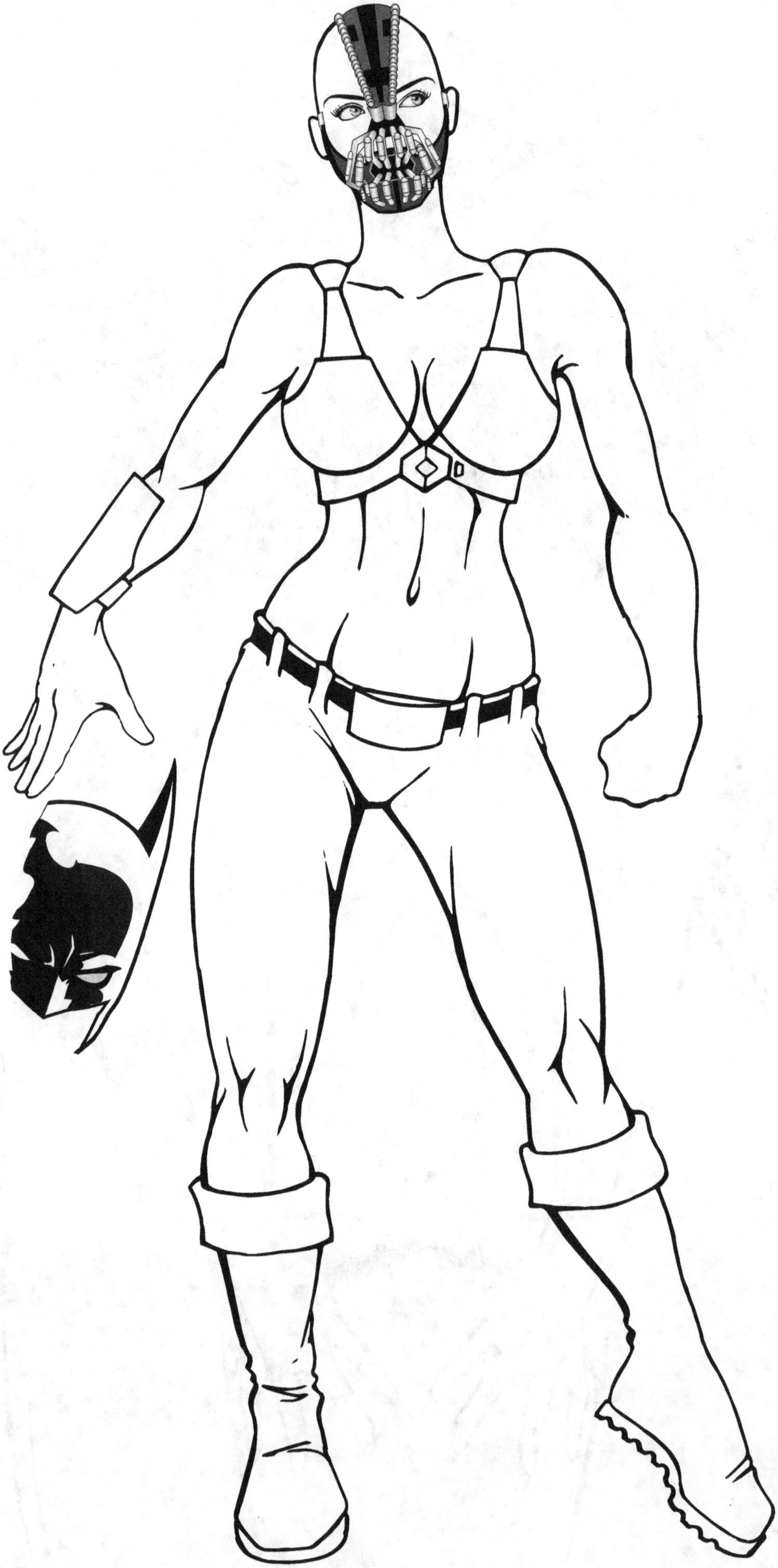

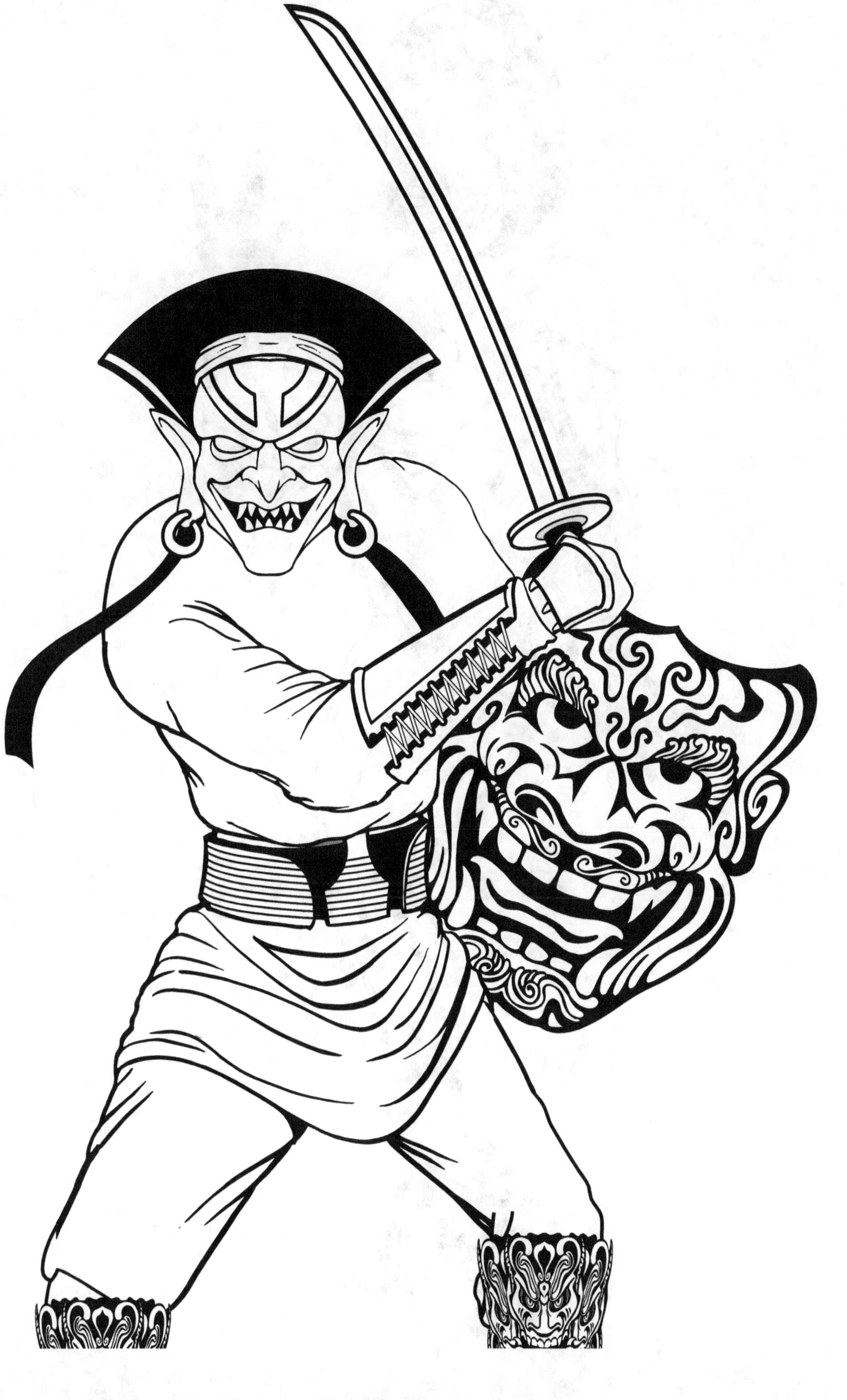

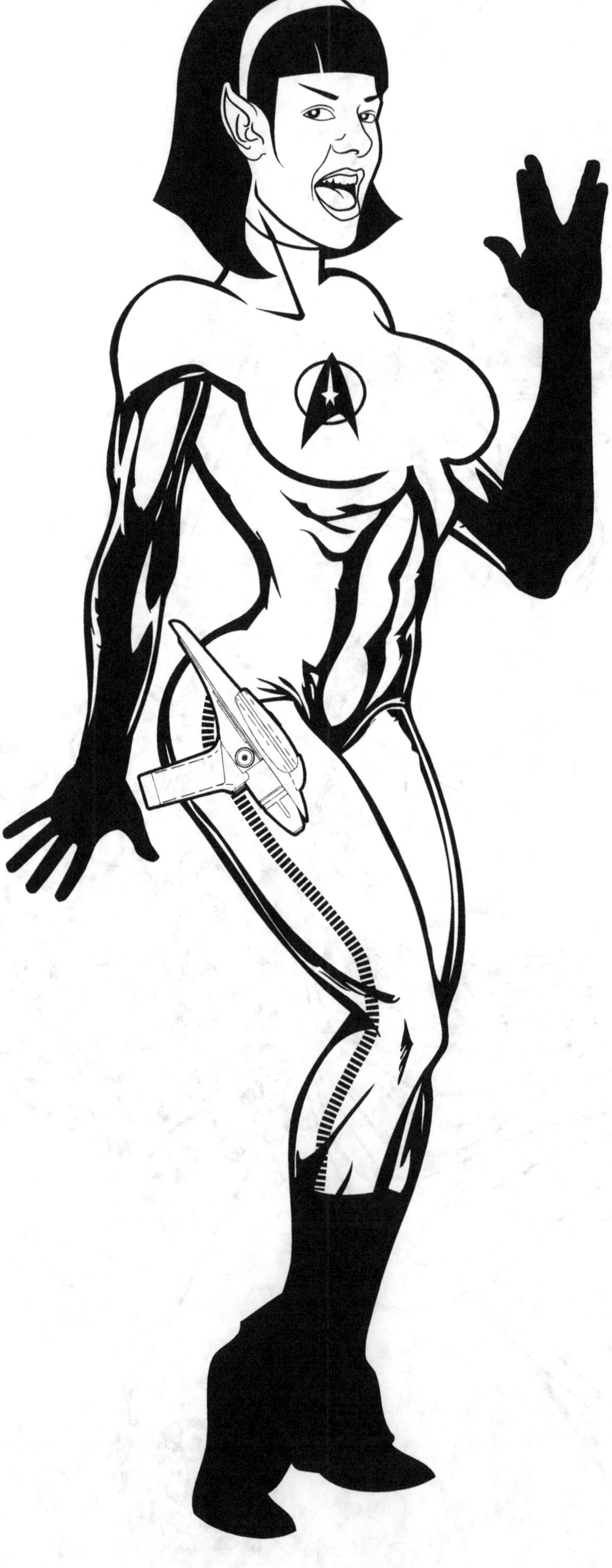

TIKI-Ty

COLORiNG BOOKS

www.ingramcontent.com/pod-product-compliance
Lightning Source LLC
Chambersburg PA
CBHW081311180526
45170CB00007B/2654
* 9 7 8 1 5 2 3 2 8 3 9 3 4 *